eliane

Food to make the soul smile

by Rafia Willmott & Anna Fidler

THANK YOU

We want to say a big thank you firstly to the brilliant
team at Eliane. They have seen the restaurant grow
and evolve and have got through the teething problems
and the successes with humour and grace. Thank you
for helping us to continue to provide the kind of service
our customers deserve.

To our lovely friends and families who have supported
and helped us all the way. They have been our greatest
champions but have also cared enough to be honest
when things are not as perfect as they could be!
Every recipe has passed this test and we cannot thank
them enough for making sure that we are at our best.

Finally, to our fantastic customers, thank you for talking
to us, giving us feedback, making suggestions and sharing
your delight when we get things right. We would be nothing
without you and we value your support, please keep
coming back!

DESIGNED BY S&T Design
sandtdesign.co.uk

PRINTED BY – 1010 Printing International Ltd, China
ISBN NO. 978-0-9571699-1-3
PUBLISHED BY – elianesmiles

Contents

Anyone raising a family would tell you that catering to everyone's individual needs and preferences is hardly the simplest of tasks. No matter how great you are in the kitchen, family always seem to balance appreciating your cooking with telling you how you can improve! But it is their opinions that shape how one develops culinary skills and cooking ideas.

Over the years, having developed many styles of cooking from cultures all over the world, we have found that making dishes adaptable to almost any palate is not as hard a job as one might expect. It only requires a little knowledge of ingredients, flavours and some imagination, and suddenly anything is possible.

This recipe book is a compilation of some of our favourite and most popular recipes from the restaurant, with some new ones as well. The recipes are health conscious, and the book is structured into four sections depending on what type of dish you are looking to prepare and what your objectives are. So, if you're looking for delicious foods for entertaining, watching weight, to nourish and heal, or simply to indulge, then just like at our restaurant, you'll be spoilt for choice!

Rafia Willmott

In 2014, in partnership with Mark, one of my closest friends, we embarked on bringing some of our knowledge of food and preparation to the public. We opened our first ever restaurant in Hungerford, West Berkshire, with the concept being 'Choices'. The restaurant's objective is to ensure that everyone and anyone can be catered for irrespective of their tastes, beliefs, ethics or dietary restrictions. The concept of Choices was borne out of knowing that in my family alone, everyone was an individual with differing preferences and so finding a restaurant that everyone is a hundred per cent happy with might not always be easily done. So the idea of creating a healthy eating establishment that serves a wide range of speciality dishes, where everyone can find something to meet their requirements would almost certainly be a hit. We were right!

The recipes you'll see here have been collaborated on with my good friend Anna, who has been with me the whole way from the opening of the first Eliane restaurant. Also together with Mark, who has been there to advise me and my staff on food preparation and on the ingredients that we choose - all from a health perspective.

The reason for me wanting to create this recipe book was to empower the home cook with options for the whole family. I wanted to bring several eating styles to one book so if there's an allergy sufferer in your family or a vegan, vegetarian, raw foodist or just a fussy eater, a recipe book that covers practically all bases would be a valuable tool in the varied modern-day kitchen. I am thrilled to say that it has been a labour of love to create this book, and to have done it in collaboration with some of my closest friends has been a blessing.

I hope you enjoy!

Rafia

Anna Fidler

I started my career in catering at the early age of thirteen working in my maternal grandmother's restaurant. Over the next three decades I tended bar in the stylish eateries of Lan Kwai Fong in Hong Kong, catered for hundreds of guests at weddings, ran a deli, wrote a cookbook and provided meals for hungry stars and crew on locations for music videos and photo shoots. These experiences, along with living on four continents, have created a diverse collection of food memories that have become part of my culinary DNA.

My interest in healthy eating started when I first lived away from home as a student in the 1980s. A group of friends made a conscious decision to eat a vegetarian diet with no processed food and only natural sugars. We made everything from scratch using homegrown and organic produce, with no additives or preservatives - a very unusual choice at the time. This combination of culinary influences and creative cooking provided a great platform for my work at Eliane.

After Rafia and I met, our friendship blossomed through a common bond when it comes to food. We have a passion for creating dishes that explore ingredients from all over the world, and I have definitely met my match when it comes to setting the highest standards for how food looks and tastes! I wanted to write this book to celebrate what we have achieved at Eliane and to show a wider audience that healthy food can look and taste amazing. There is no better feeling than bringing people together and nurturing them with good food and great company.

Working together with such creative, beautiful people and developing new friendships has been an absolute joy.

Lots of love

Anna

Mark Kimchi

Mark and I co-founded the first Eliane restaurant from a vision of being able to help people with dietary-specific needs. He is a researcher of food science in relation to diseases and consults with individuals to correct their diets from his private practice in Bedfordshire. He also runs courses in raw food preparation.

His involvement with the restaurant and contribution to this recipe book has been to introduce the raw vegan options that many are turning to for health and wellbeing today. Some of Mark's recipes feature exclusively at Eliane, and all the staff adhere to the strict guidelines for food preparation that he has trained them all in.

In early 2016, Mark opened Raw Respite, an organic vegan retreat - the first of its kind - incorporating bespoke programs for individuals comprising cleanses, detoxes and workshops.

www.natureistheanswer.com
www.rawrespite.com

Rodney Love

Rodney is one of my greatest friends. He's been my spiritual inspiration for 24 years.

He is a fine artist from the UK who, late in life, found the partnership of the digital camera and the computer a beguiling set of tools to explore his passion for colour, shape and form.

In the past 20 years of working in this medium, selectively teaching himself the various editing programmes as they have appeared on the market, Rodney has evolved his style while taking on board the continuing possibilities these creative spring boards allow.

Rodney's work has been commissioned for private collections and shown in New Zealand, Australia, the UK and France. He currently lives and creates images in the South of France.

Working on the Eliane cookbook was a challenge in itself as it was a new and unexplored area for him to apply his vision and appreciation of all things colourful, and in this case, also very tasty!

Rodney's work can be seen here:
www.ello.co/rodneylove

place

et and eat ●

&...

With food that not only tastes good but that nourishes you as well, our goal is accomplished…

…We know that eating healthily might not seem appetising to most, but at Eliane, achieving taste without compromising nutrition is what we do best. We source the best quality ingredients we can find, infusing our passion for creating unique and delicious, vibrant and health-giving foods that everyone can enjoy.

This cookbook has been created as an extension of what we do at Eliane. It shows you how you can achieve and perfect these dishes at home, putting a lot of smiles on a lot of faces at your dinner table.

The Heal section has been largely contributed to by Mark Kimchi, the co-founder of Eliane. Mark is also the founder of Raw Respite - a fully organic, raw vegan luxury retreat on the border of Bedfordshire's countryside. The retreat itself is privately owned and managed by Mark.
The retreat offers courses and workshops together with overnight, week-long and full month stays catering to any needs from beginning a road to recovery from disease, to detoxes, full cleanses and some simple respite from city life. Retreats can be tailor-made to specifically suit individual requirements, and all stays include a consultation with Mark himself.
www.rawrespite.com

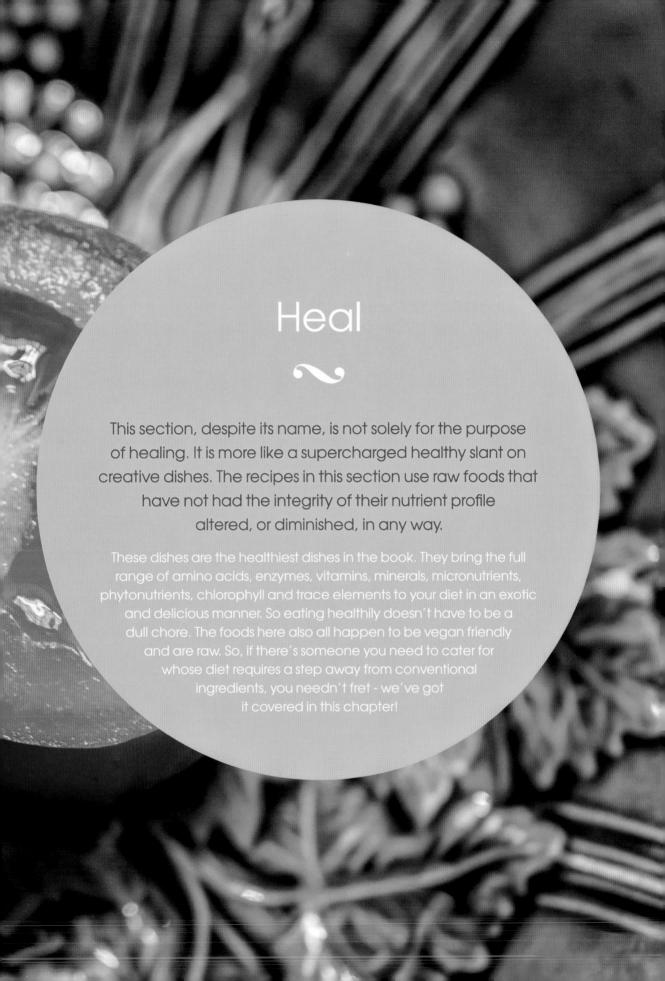

Heal

❧

This section, despite its name, is not solely for the purpose of healing. It is more like a supercharged healthy slant on creative dishes. The recipes in this section use raw foods that have not had the integrity of their nutrient profile altered, or diminished, in any way.

These dishes are the healthiest dishes in the book. They bring the full range of amino acids, enzymes, vitamins, minerals, micronutrients, phytonutrients, chlorophyll and trace elements to your diet in an exotic and delicious manner. So eating healthily doesn't have to be a dull chore. The foods here also all happen to be vegan friendly and are raw. So, if there's someone you need to cater for whose diet requires a step away from conventional ingredients, you needn't fret - we've got it covered in this chapter!

*Avocados provide almost 20 essential
nutrients, including fibre, potassium,
vitamin E, B vitamins, folic acid
and many more micronutrients.
Collectively, the avocado's composition
actually functions as a 'nutrient booster'.
This means it enables the body to absorb
more fat-soluble nutrients in foods
that are eaten with this fruit, such as
alpha and beta-carotine and lutein.*

Avocado with pink grapefruit, chilli & pine nuts

Serves 4 as a side salad

_____

1 pink grapefruit

3 ripe avocados

1 tsp chilli flakes or 1 small red chilli, finely chopped

a drizzle of cold pressed extra virgin olive oil

a little Himalayan pink salt

a handful of pine nuts

This is the simplest of salads to make but looks really appetising. The citrusy tang of the grapefruit, with a pop of chilli, really complements the creaminess of the avocado.

Cut the peel from the pink grapefruit, making sure you remove all the pith. Now segment the fruit by running a sharp knife down the sides of each segment, towards the core of the grapefruit - follow the lines of the membranes that separate each one. I know that this is laborious, but it makes a huge difference to the final taste and texture, as the pith and membrane can be fibrous and bitter.

Cut the segments in half and toss in a bowl with a little of the juice. Slice the avocado into thin slices and gently mix in with the grapefruit; the acidity of the juice will stop the avocado going brown.

Sprinkle over the chilli and salt, drizzle with olive oil and scatter over the pine nuts.

Beetroot, orange, caper & pistachio salad

Serves 4-6 as a side salad

———

2 large or 3-4 small bulbs of raw beetroot, washed and peeled (if necessary)

2 sweet oranges

1 purple endive

4-6 tbsp capers, drained weight

½ small red onion, finely sliced

3-4 tbsp unfiltered, cold pressed extra virgin olive oil

1-2 tbsp raw, unfiltered apple cider vinegar

a handful of pistachio nuts, roughly chopped

Himalayan pink salt and pepper to taste

The earthy sweetness of the beetroot is matched beautifully by the zingy tang from the oranges and the sharp saltiness of the capers. A great raw salad to add colour to a party menu and, for those not on a raw vegan diet, a perfect accompaniment to smoked fish or roasted vegetables for a light lunch.

Roughly grate the raw beetroot (in a food processor or julienned with a mandolin, if you prefer larger strips). Squeeze any excess beet juice into a bowl and reserve (use this for your dressing and drink any that is left over!). Then segment the oranges; trim off each end, cut off the skin just below the pith and then slide a knife down the pith membrane to release each segment. Transfer the segments, with any juice, to the grated beetroot.

Cut the endive in half, separate the leaves and keep whole, or thinly slice, then add to the beetroot and orange.

Finally, add all the remaining ingredients and toss together gently. Taste, adjust the seasoning and serve.

Full of nitrates, the beetroot has roughly 20 times more than most other vegetables. Nitrates help improve the efficiency of the processes that occur in the mitochondria, known as the cell's energy factory. Simply put, this means beetroots provide your cells with energy!

Cashew cheese & raw dips

Cashew cheese

120g raw cashew nuts

approx 60ml filtered water

30g nutritional yeast*

2 tbsp fresh lemon juice

2 cloves garlic

1 tbsp raw, unfiltered apple cider vinegar

1 tbsp Dijon mustard

Himalayan pink salt and pepper to taste

Cashews are heavy on the omega 6s, but eaten in moderation are a great source of magnesium and copper. They are wonderfully versatile in dishes such as these!

Cashew cheese is a perfect vegan alternative to a soft cream cheese. Great as a spread or to add a creamy texture to raw dips. Omit the Dijon mustard and you have a perfect cream cheese alternative to make a vegan cheesecake!

Start by soaking the cashew nuts overnight in plenty of cold water. When ready to make the cheese, drain off the cashew nuts and simply put the nuts, half the filtered water and all the other ingredients into a food processor and blend until thick and creamy. The texture should be similar to a smooth hummus. If the mixture is too thick, add a little more of the filtered water that you have in reserve. Once blended to the correct consistency, spoon into a container and place in the fridge. The cheese will harden when chilled.

Try adding chopped fresh herbs, cracked black pepper or red chilli to make any number of variations.

*Nutritional yeast has a strong flavour that is described as nutty, cheesy or creamy, which makes it popular as an ingredient in vegan recipes in place of cheese. It can also be used as a flavouring in stocks, soups, sauces etc.

Bombay spiced dip

1 portion of cashew cheese
(as per recipe opposite)

½ tsp ground turmeric

½ tsp garam masala

½ chilli, deseeded and finely
chopped (optional)

a little almond or coconut milk

a small handful of fresh
coriander, chopped

a little Himalayan pink salt
and pepper

Mix together all the ingredients
with enough almond milk to
loosen off the mixture to a
dipping consistency, similar
to a thick hummus.
Season and serve.

Beetroot and walnut dip

½ portion of cashew cheese
(as per recipe opposite)

1 medium beetroot bulb,
peeled and roughly chopped

½ red onion, roughly chopped

juice of half a lemon

approx 6-8 tbsp cold pressed
extra virgin olive oil

3-4 tbsp fresh flat leaf parsley,
chopped

50g walnuts

1 tbsp raw, unfiltered apple
cider vinegar

½ tsp nutmeg

a little Himalayan pink salt
and pepper

Place all the ingredients in a high
speed blender until smooth.
Season and serve.

Thai spice and coconut dip

½ portion of cashew cheese
(as per recipe opposite)

1 ripe avocado

1-2 tsp Thai green curry paste
(see page 222)

a small handful of fresh coriander

a little coconut milk

a little Himalayan pink salt
and pepper

Spoon the cashew cheese into
a blender. Add the avocado
(if very ripe, just remove the stone
and squeeze the flesh out), the
curry paste, coriander and a
splash of coconut milk. Blend until
smooth, adding more coconut
milk if necessary. Season and serve.
The amount of curry paste you
add is entirely dependent on
how hot you like it.

*Coriander is a wonderful herb
for heart health, regulation of
blood sugar and digestion. It is
also a mild antimicrobial herb
and diuretic, so it can assist with
treating infections, such as in
the urinary tract.*

*Of all the nuts, walnuts possess
a much more balanced ratio of
omega 6s to 3s, making them a
nut of choice if looking to feed
your brain!*

*Lemongrass (an ingredient of Thai
green curry paste) is also dubbed as
'Fever Grass' because of its medicinal
qualities used to treat a host of
digestion issues. It is used to enhance
the flavour of the dishes in Asian
cuisine and it has sweet and mild
taste. It contains vitamin C, A, folic
acid, foliate, magnesium, copper,
iron, zinc, potassium, calcium,
phosphorus and manganese.*

Celery salad with grapes & walnuts

Celery is rich in electrolytes and has a cooling effect on the body. It lowers oxidative stress in the heart and helps clear the digestive system. Studies also have found that celery can reduce fatty deposits in the liver.

Serves 4

_____

FOR THE CASHEW NUT MAYONNAISE:

100g raw cashew nuts

1 tbsp mustard

1-2 tsp raw, unfiltered apple cider vinegar

4-6 tbsp cold pressed extra virgin olive oil

approx 70ml freshly squeezed apple juice

1 tsp each of Himalayan pink salt & black pepper or 2 tbsp liquid aminos*

FOR THE SALAD:

3 tart apples, e.g. Granny Smith, cored and finely diced

approx 1-2 tbsp fresh lemon juice

1-2 tbsp cold pressed extra virgin olive oil

3 stalks celery, finely chopped

100g seedless grapes, halved

a pinch of of Himalayan pink salt

a good-sized handful of chopped walnuts

This salad has similar flavours to a classic Waldorf salad and is surprisingly creamy for a raw vegan version.

Start by making the cashew nut mayonnaise. Soak the nuts in plenty of cold water for at least 2 hours, preferably overnight. Drain the nuts and blend with all the ingredients, except the apple juice. Once the mixture is smooth, add enough apple juice to create a thick and creamy mayonnaise. Stir through the Himalayan pink salt and pepper or the liquid aminos*, check the seasoning, adding more if necessary, and set aside until needed.

To finish off the salad, take a large serving bowl and toss the chopped apples with lemon juice and oil. Stir in the celery, grapes and enough cashew nut mayonnaise to coat the salad wel. Chill until needed. Taste and season the salad with a little salt, place mixed leaves onto a large platter top with the finished salad, sprinkle with walnuts and serve.

For a lighter version, omit the cashew mayonnaise and simply add a little raw, unfiltered apple cider vinegar and cold pressed extra virgin olive oil, and season with Himalayan pink salt and pepper.

*The most common form of liquid aminos is made by Braggs. It offers a number of the essential amino acids we all need in our diet (these come predominantly from animal proteins but are also found in pulses and beans). In a raw diet, liquid aminos offer an alternative way of getting these essential amino acids (although in low doses). Liquid aminos are also a wheat-free alternative to soy sauce and make a useful flavour enhancer.

Citrus & date salad

The Romans viewed the fennel plant as the herb of eyesight. In addition, root extracts were used to clear cloudy eyes. Fennel seeds have also been found in tests to destroy various cancerous cell growths. Fennel also has a high content of antioxidants, which play an important role in eliminating and preventing cancer cells.

Serves 4-6

FOR THE DRESSING:

1 tsp cumin seeds

1 tsp fennel seeds

5 tbsp cold pressed extra virgin olive oil

a pinch of Himalayan pink salt and black pepper

2 garlic cloves, crushed

¼ tsp cardamom powder

¼ tsp cinnamon powder

1 tsp orange blossom water

FOR THE SALAD:

6 medium oranges

1 red onion, thinly sliced

6 medjool dates, pitted and sliced

150g radishes, thinly sliced

a small handful each of fresh coriander, parsley and mint, chopped

a dozen small pitted olives (optional)

2 large handfuls of rocket and watercress leaves (optional)

Start by toasting the fennel and cumin seeds in a dry frying pan over a medium heat, being careful not to let them burn; you just want to release the flavours. For a purely raw salad, do not toast the seeds. Crush the toasted (or raw) seeds in a pestle and mortar and then mix together all of the dressing ingredients in a large bowl and whisk until emulsified.

Slice off the skin of the oranges, making sure the majority of the pith is removed. Now take a sharp knife and gently slide down each of the membrane pockets to release the orange segment. This is a little laborious, but the pith and membrane are tough and bitter. The taste and texture of the salad will really benefit from this extra work.

Now take the thinly sliced onion and tip it into the bowl. With your hands, massage the dressing into the onion; this will soften some of the sharpness and pungency of the onion. Once this is done, gently fold in the remaining ingredients, season and serve.

Courgette noodles with tomato & herb sauce

Serves 3-4 as a main salad

———

4 small courgettes

½ red bell pepper, julienned into thin strips

FOR THE SUNDRIED TOMATO SAUCE:

60g sundried tomatoes, dry packed - not in oil

2 cloves garlic, crushed

1 tbsp cold pressed extra virgin olive oil

1 ripe avocado

a small handful of fresh basil leaves

1 tbsp raw, unfiltered apple cider vinegar

½ tbsp lemon juice

¼ tsp dried oregano

a pinch of Himalayan pink salt and pepper

as an alternative, try a spicy Thai sauce for the noodles:

FOR THE THAI SAUCE:

1 tbsp raw almond butter (or peanut butter)

½ tbsp raw, unfiltered apple cider vinegar

½ tbsp gluten-free Tamari soy sauce (or liquid aminos)

1 to 2 cloves garlic, crushed or minced

a small handful of fresh basil, roughly chopped

a small handful of fresh coriander, roughly chopped

½ a chilli, deseeded and chopped

½ tsp raw sesame oil

½ tsp grated fresh ginger

1 lemongrass stalk, chopped finely and crushed

Wash the courgettes well and trim off their ends. Using a spiralizer or a mandolin, turn the courgettes into thin strips or 'noodles'. Line a large serving bowl with paper towel, or a clean tea towel (this will help to absorb the moisture released from the courgettes). Then place the courgette noodles in the bowl along with the strips of red bell pepper and set aside.

For the tomato and herb sauce
Place the sundried tomato, garlic, olive oil and the avocado in a food processor. Next, add the basil, apple cider vinegar, lemon juice, oregano and salt. Blend all the ingredients to a smooth, thick purée. Season and set aside.

For the spicy Thai sauce
In a small bowl, whisk the almond butter with ½ tbsp of water and all remaining ingredients. If the mixture is hard to combine, add a little more water. The sauce should be quite thick. Be careful not to make it too runny as the courgette noodles will continue to release moisture once the sauce is added.

Remove the towels from under the courgette and pepper mix and add either the tomato and herb or the spicy Thai sauce, stirring well to coat the noodles completely and serve right away. Any leftovers can be refrigerated, but water will continue to seep from the courgettes into the sauce, so make sure to drain a little of the excess liquid off and stir well before serving.

———

Courgettes do wonders for your waistline; very low in calories and they have a perfect texture for raw dishes. They contain no saturated fats and the peel is rich in dietary fibre. Courgettes have high levels of antioxidants as well.

Flavoured apple cider water

Serves 4-6

___

APPLE AND MINT:

1 litre of filtered water

4 tbsp raw, unfiltered apple cider vinegar

1-2 apples, thinly sliced

approx 10 mint leaves, torn

RED BERRY:

1 litre of filtered water

4 tbsp raw, unfiltered apple cider vinegar

a large handful of fresh or frozen berries: strawberry, raspberry, cherry, blackberry etc

LEMON AND CUCUMBER:

1 litre of filtered water

4 tbsp raw, unfiltered apple cider vinegar

½ cucumber, thinly sliced

juice of 1-2 lemons

Mixing the apple cider vinegar with water and infusing it with fruit and herbs makes a very refreshing and palatable drink. Try other variations to find one that suits you. Here are a few recipes that we use in the restaurant. Just mix all the ingredients together and chill for at least 20 minutes before serving.

Unfiltered and unpasteurised organic apple cider vinegar has many proven and anecdotal health benefits. Many believe that it is the 'mother', the strands of proteins, enzymes and friendly bacteria, found in this type of vinegar that maximises any benefits it may bring. Studies have shown that this vinegar, when ingested, has an effect on stabilising blood sugar levels and regulating insulin production, as well as increasing our feeling of fullness. All of these factors are very important in helping us not to over eat and in balancing our blood sugar levels. Other benefits include lowering cholesterol and blood pressure and helping to fight cancer.

Homemade lemonade

Serves 4-6

———

3-4 whole, unwaxed lemons
(if you have a juicer)

juice from 4-7 lemons, around 225ml
(if you are making by hand)

1 litre filtered water

100-150g coconut nectar

Very refreshing and very simple to make. Adjust the lemonade to your liking - some may like the lemonade tarter or sweeter; just adjust the amount of coconut nectar or the number of lemons.

Once you have perfected the basic recipe, you can try any number of variations: use limes and fresh mint to make a virgin mojito, try adding some pink grapefruit juice or raspberries to make pink lemonade or infuse with thinly sliced cucumber and sprigs of rosemary for something that looks, and tastes, a bit different.

Start by juicing 3-4 whole lemons, including the skin (if you do not have a juicer, simply pour the freshly squeezed lemon juice into a large jug). Then blend all the other ingredients together with the lemon juice, check the flavour and add more lemon juice or coconut nectar, if needed. Serve over ice.

Lemons, despite being acidic, are actually highly alkalising once inside the body. They stimulate incredible all-round health by promoting the correct pH levels in the blood - which is a major disease-preventative. Lemons are great for skin, hair and digestion too.

Cumin is referred to as a carminative, which means that it relieves you from gas troubles, and improves digestion and appetite. The essential oils of cumin, coupled with its magnesium and sodium content, promotes easier digestion and also gives relief for stomach aches.

Mushroom with celery, herbs & shallots

Serves 4-6

———

approx 800g chestnut and button mushrooms

½ shallot, finely chopped

3 tbsp cold pressed extra virgin olive oil

2 tbsp fresh lemon juice

1 tsp unwaxed lemon zest

1 tbsp coconut nectar

¼ - ½ tsp cayenne pepper

2 small garlic cloves, crushed

1 tsp ground cumin

200g edamame or broad beans (fresh or defrosted from frozen)

2 stalks celery, finely sliced

90-100g hazelnuts, chopped

80g walnut pieces, roughly chopped

4-5 tbsp tahini paste

a small handful each of fresh flat leaf parsley and coriander, chopped

Himalayan pink salt and pepper to taste

Wash and dry the mushrooms and slice about 1cm thick. Place in a medium-sized serving bowl with the shallots. Whisk together the oil, lemon juice, lemon zest, coconut nectar, cayenne pepper, garlic and cumin. Toss this dressing through the mushroom and shallot mixture and refrigerate for at least 30 minutes, stirring every 10 minutes or so. The oil and lemon will draw moisture out of the mushrooms, giving them a denser, more earthy flavour.

While the mushrooms are marinading, prepare the other ingredients; if using broad beans, check to see if the outer hull is too hard. Remove the outer hull from the broad beans, if necessary. Pour the edamame or broad beans into a large bowl and gently crush the beans with a potato masher, or the back of a fork. Into the crushed beans, stir the celery, nuts, tahini paste and herbs.

Once the mushrooms are well marinated, remove them from the fridge and drain off any excess liquid and reserve. Mix the mushrooms into the bean and tahini salad, adding enough of the reserved liquid to moisten the dish. Season with salt and pepper and a splash more lemon juice, if necessary, and serve.

"The doctor of the future will no longer treat the human frame with drugs, but rather will cure and prevent disease with nutrition."
Thomas Edison

Mushrooms with kohlrabi & herbs

**Serves 4 as a main dish,
6-8 as a side**

_____

1-2 shallots, finely chopped

2 kohlrabi bulbs, peeled and
thinly julienned

4-5 tbsp coconut nectar

5-6 tbsp raw, unfiltered apple
cider vinegar

approx 400g button mushrooms,
washed and thinly sliced

½ tsp Himalayan pink salt
and pepper

a handful of fresh flat leaf parsley,
chopped

a small handful of fresh mint,
chopped

5-6 tbsp cold pressed extra virgin
olive oil

1 small bunch of spring onions,
chopped

3-4 tbsp raw pumpkin seeds

3-4 tbsp pomegranate seeds

Soak shallots and kohlrabi in the coconut nectar and apple cider
vinegar for an hour and then mix together all of the ingredients in
a large bowl with your hands.

Season and serve with a sprinkle of pumpkin and pomegranate seeds.

*Kohlrabi is a
mineral and fibre-rich
vegetable. It is particularly
high in iron and potassium, which
goes some way to improve nerve
and muscle function and prevent
anaemia. Kohlrabi is a member
of the cabbage family but is
somewhat more palatable
and versatile in dishes.*

No excuse... it's time to juice!

Boost Juice - The combination of cucumber and celery in this juice is a wonderful pH balancer. Owing to their water-rich content, the hydration available from this juice is fantastic.

Wakey Wakey - An easy way to get the benefits of lots of carrots into your diet. Carrots make the skin glow, improve eye vision and strengthen teeth and gums.

Bloody Marvelous - Beetroot juice is, surprisingly, a brilliant pre or post workout drink. It indirectly dramatically increases the energy available to the cells because it causes less of a need for oxygen consumption by the cells.

Each recipe makes approx 250ml (1 cup) of juice

BOOST JUICE
hydrating and cleansing:

½ a cucumber

1-2 stalks of celery

1cm (½") chunk of fresh ginger

1-2 apples

2 sprigs of fresh mint

WAKEY WAKEY
hydrating and enlivening:

4-5 carrots

2 apples

1-2 oranges

BLOODY MARVELOUS
hydrating and satiating:

2 beetroot bulbs

1-2 apples

3-4 carrots

¼ lemon

Juicing is the perfect way to get a boost of vitamins and minerals into your system. A juicer is an essential piece of kit, and the sky's the limit when it comes to price. To get you started, buy a simple, cheap model (£30 should cover it!). That way you can experiment and see if it is something you love. Although, once you've started there's no turning back. Whether you're someone who needs a nutrient injection in the mornings to get you up and out, or you have teenagers who seem to survive on nothing but junk food, or toddlers who clamp their mouths shut at the sight of a carrot, juicing is the answer!

Try to use organic fruit and vegetables, but if you can't, wash everything in a solution of water and apple cider vinegar. This will remove residues from the surface as, generally, we juice the fruit or vegetable whole. Citrus fruit is the only exception, as the skins can be quite bitter and, in large quantities, can damage the juicer. Experiment and see what you enjoy.

To make your juice, wash the fruit and/or vegetables, cut into chunks that will fit into the feeder of your juicer, and juice! You can adapt recipes to suit your palate, adding more or less of the stronger ingredients such as lemon or ginger. Most fruits have a higher calorific value than vegetables, so, if you're trying to lose weight, make sure you use more vegetables. For example, carrots have a natural sweetness and work really well with apples and oranges to make a vegetable-packed juice (especially good for small people who don't like their vegetables!).

Pea & mint soup

Serves 4

approx 225ml water

½ avocado, peeled

1 clove garlic, peeled

approx 300g frozen peas
(no need to defrost)

2 handfuls spinach leaves, washed

1 tbsp lemon juice

1-2 tbsp chopped fresh mint

a little Himalayan pink salt and
pepper to taste

Pour all of the ingredients in a blender and blend until smooth.
Adjust the seasoning and serve.

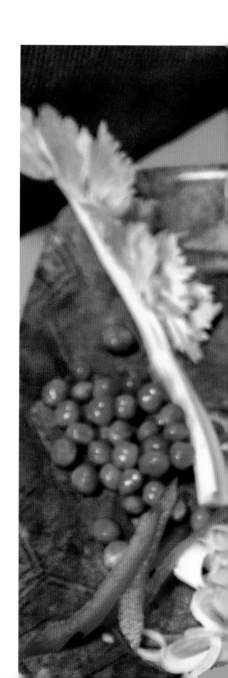

Mint is traditionally thought of as being good for digestion and keeping the breath fresh, but mint has also been shown to improve mental alertness and memory retention, which are attributable to mint's natural stimulant properties.

A sprinkling of oregano in your meals can seriously improve your immune health. Two of the most important constituents of oregano are thymol and rosmarinic acid, both of which are powerful antioxidant compounds that can reduce oxidative stress in the body.

Raw lasagna

Serves 2-4

_____

4 medium-sized courgettes

2 plum tomatoes, finely sliced

2 avocados, peeled and finely sliced

50g fresh coconut, finely sliced

FOR THE CASHEW & HAZELNUT SPREAD:

100g raw cashew nuts

100g raw hazelnuts

90ml cold, filtered water

2 tbsp nutritional yeast flakes

2 large cloves garlic, peeled and crushed

2 tbsp cold pressed extra virgin olive oil

1-2 tbsp fresh lemon juice

¼ tsp ground mustard seeds

¼ tsp Himalayan pink salt

a pinch of fresh ground black pepper

2 tbsp fresh parsley, chopped

2 tbsp fresh basil, chopped

FOR THE SUNDRIED TOMATO SAUCE:

60g sundried tomatoes, dry packed - not in oil

2 cloves garlic, peeled and crushed

1 tbsp cold pressed extra virgin olive oil

1 ripe avocado

a small handful of fresh basil leaves

1 tbsp raw, unfiltered apple cider vinegar

½ tbsp lemon juice

¼ tsp dried oregano

a pinch of Himalayan pink salt

a small handful of raw pine nuts

Start by soaking the cashews and hazelnuts in a bowl - cover the nuts with approximately a centimetre of water. Set aside to soak for an hour. Slice courgette in half crossways. You will have 8 pieces of courgette. Now slice each piece lengthwise into ½cm slices. A mandolin works well to make even slices, but slicing by hand is fine too. Set the courgette slices to one side.

For the cashew and hazelnut spread
Drain all the water from the nuts. Place the nuts, filtered water, nutritional yeast flakes, garlic, olive oil, 1 tsp lemon juice, ground mustard seeds, salt and pepper into a food processor. Process to a smooth, creamy consistency. Taste and add in a little more lemon juice, if necessary, followed by the chopped herbs. Blitz the mixture for 5-10 seconds, or until well combined and smooth.

For the sundried tomato sauce
Place the sundried tomato, garlic, olive oil and the avocado in a food processor. Next, add the basil, apple cider vinegar, lemon juice, oregano and salt. Blend all the ingredients to a smooth, thick purée. Season and set aside.

To assemble the lasagna
Line a small, oblong casserole dish with cling film. Place two of the long courgette slices next to one another, edges touching. Using the back of a spoon or an offset spatula, spread 1 tbsp of the tomato sauce over the courgette. Lay on two slices of tomato and spread 2 tbsp of the cashew nut spread. Then add two slices of the avocado and spread over 2 tbsp of the tomato sauce; repeat with alternate layers of courgette, tomatoes and avocado and alternate layers of the tomato sauce and cashew spread. As you build up the layers, occasionally add in a layer of the fresh coconut. Wrap the cling film tightly over the top of the lasagna and rest in the fridge for an hour. When ready to serve, lift it out of the dish and slide onto a platter. Garnish the top of the lasagna with pine nuts and serve immediately.

Raw Thai curry with cauliflower rice

Ginger is a wonder spice! Fresh is best, and it has been shown to be an effective anti-inflammatory. It can also help fight infections, improve brain function, fight and prevent cancer, lower cholesterol, lower blood sugar and reduce muscle soreness after exercise.

Serves 4 as a main dish

FOR THE RAW THAI CURRY PASTE:

1 tbsp raw almond butter

½ tbsp raw, unfiltered apple cider vinegar

½ tbsp gluten-free Tamari soy sauce

1 to 2 cloves garlic, crushed and finely minced

a small handful of fresh basil, roughly chopped

a small handful of fresh coriander, roughly chopped

½ -1 chilli, deseeded and finely chopped

½ tsp raw sesame oil

½ tsp grated fresh ginger

1 lemongrass stalk, chopped finely and crushed

FOR THE CURRY:

100g per person of prepared raw vegetables (peas, bell peppers etc)

FOR THE RICE:

approx ¼ - ½ a head of cauliflower per person

2-3 tbsp fresh peas per person

In a small bowl, whisk the nut butter with ½ tbsp of water and all the remaining curry paste ingredients. If the mixture is hard to combine, add a little more water but be careful not to make the sauce too runny. Add the prepared vegetables to the curry sauce and set aside until needed.

Either chop the cauliflower into rice-sized nibs, or pulse gently in a food processor until you have a rice-like consistency. Stir through the peas and season to taste.

Check and season the Thai curry and serve alongside the cauliflower rice. Serve immediately

Dill has many benefits, but one that is little heard of is how it can reduce the associated pain of diseases such as gout and rheumatoid arthritis. Dill has in fact been used since ancient times for precisely this purpose.

Raw winter vegetable salad

Serves 6 as a main dish

---

1 small bulb of celeriac and swede, both peeled and julienned into thin strips

a small handful each of flat leaf parsley and dill, chopped

approx 6 tbsp capers, drained and roughly chopped

juice of a lemon

3 tsp wholegrain mustard

8 tbsp cold pressed extra virgin olive oil

3 tsp raw, unfiltered apple cider vinegar

3 tsp coconut nectar

approx 150g of dried cranberries and/or raisins

1 small pointed green cabbage, finely shredded

a small handful of pumpkin seeds

a little extra fresh herb, parsley is perfect, to decorate

Place the celeriac and swede into a large bowl, add all the other ingredients (except the cabbage) and massage the vegetables by hand; this will gently bruise them, allowing the other ingredients to be absorbed. Taste and adjust the seasoning, making sure there is plenty of dressing in the bowl.

The salad can now be left until needed; overnight is perfect. Just before serving, toss through the finely shredded cabbage. This gives a fresh crunchy texture to add to the sweet and sour earthiness of the root vegetables.

To serve, scatter over some pumpkin seeds and freshly chopped herbs.

Red cabbage with dates & orange

Serves 4

———

2 oranges

½ small red cabbage

approx 6 dates, pitted and sliced

3 spring onions, thinly sliced

½ tsp fennel seeds

2 tbsp cold pressed extra virgin
olive oil

small handful of fresh mint, chopped

1 tsp white sesame seeds

a pinch of Himalayan pink salt
and pepper

1-2 tbsp pistachio nuts,
roughly chopped

Start by preparing the oranges. Slice off the skin and pith and, holding the orange over a bowl to preserve the juices, remove each orange segment from its pithy outer layer. This may seem like a laborious task, but the pith can be very bitter and will end up overpowering the flavours of the salad.

Remove a few of the outer cabbage leaves and reserve. Then slice the cabbage into very thin strips, either with a sharp knife or a mandolin.

Crush the fennel seeds in a pestle and mortar and add to the red cabbage. Pour over the reserved orange juice and gently massage together; this will start to soften the strands of cabbage.

Add in all the other ingredients, except the pistachio nuts, and mix well with your hands. Season, sprinkle over the pistachio nuts and serve piled into the reserved cabbage leaves or in a large bowl.

Sesame seeds contain appreciable amounts of zinc, a vital component in the formation of collagen, which strengthens muscle tissue, hair and skin. Sesame seeds also contain phytate, an unusual cancer-preventing compound that reduces the impact and effects of free radicals through its antioxidant function.

Spicy vegetable wraps

The humble lettuce leaf often gets thought of as 'nutrient-light', but it is in fact quite the opposite. Apart from lowering cholesterol, having a range of free-radical fighting properties, helping to induce restful sleep and having antimicrobial compounds, extracts of lettuce have been shown to protect brain cells from some neurodegenerative diseases. Quite the leaf!

Serves 4 as a main dish

approx 12 whole, soft lettuce leaves, such as a classic round lettuce

1 red pepper, deseeded and thinly sliced

3 spring onions, thinly sliced

a small handful of bean sprouts

1 small preserved lemon, finely diced

1 medium carrot, finely diced

a small handful of fresh coriander, finely chopped

4 button mushrooms, finely diced

2 tbsp cold pressed extra virgin olive oil

2-3 tbsp raw pine nuts

a pinch of red chilli flakes (optional)

1 tsp za'atar

a pinch of Himalayan pink salt and pepper

Mix all of the ingredients together with your hands, gently massaging the vegetables to help the flavours to infuse.

When ready to eat, prepare the parcels. The choice of lettuce is dependent on personal preference and how you want the wraps to look. Choose a soft leaf if you wish to wrap or fold the lettuce around the filling, or something more robust, like endive, if you want the filling to sit into a firmer shell. Place a few tablespoons of the spicy vegetable mixture onto each of the leaves, roll or leave open and serve.

Stuffed raw mushrooms

Serves 4 as a main dish

_____

12 medium-sized chestnut mushrooms

FOR THE FILLING:

approx 150g raw cashew nuts

a small handful of fresh coriander,
roughly chopped

approx 2 tbsp fresh mint, chopped

approx 2 tbsp of fresh basil, chopped

2 cloves of garlic, peeled

1 pitted date

2 tbsp fresh lemon juice

a pinch of Himalayan pink salt
and pepper

TO DECORATE:

6 tbsp raw pine nuts

Start by wiping or washing the mushrooms to remove any dirt or debris and lay out to dry on some kitchen towel. Gently remove the stems and roughly chop.

Add all the filling ingredients, including the mushroom stems, into a food processor. Whizz everything together to create a thick paste. Season and set aside until needed.

Fill each mushroom with the filling. Decorate with the pine nuts and serve on a beautiful platter.

This recipe also makes a wonderful raw canapé. Just select small, bite-sized button mushrooms.

Mushrooms are low in calories, high in fibre, rich in potassium, folate, B vitamins and phytochemicals. The chestnut mushroom has anti-cancer properties and antifungal properties. The antioxidants present also suppress the absorption of cholesterol.

greetings

freshness

good friend

ambience

&gratitude

&choice

&laughter

&comfort

Superfood salad

Serves 4

1 red onion, finely sliced

4 tbsp raw, unfiltered apple cider vinegar

1 tbsp coconut nectar

2 whole corn on the cob

2 red bell peppers, thinly sliced

3-4 stalks of celery, chopped

a small handful each of fresh flat leaf parsley, mint and basil, chopped

1 tbsp sesame seeds

1 tsp chia seeds

1 tsp alfalfa seeds

1 tsp each of barley grass and wheatgrass powder

approx 8 tbsp cold pressed extra virgin olive oil

juice of a fresh lemon

Himalayan pink salt and pepper to taste

This raw salad can be made with any combination of organic vegetables that are available. Try using an array of nuts and seeds to change the texture and flavours.

Tip the sliced red onion into a small bowl and pour over the apple cider vinegar and coconut nectar. Massage the vinegar and nectar into the onion with a little salt. This will help to break down the onion and soften the flavours. Next, take the corn cobs and slice off the kernels with a sharp knife and tip into a large serving bowl. Add in the sliced peppers, celery, fresh herbs and all of the seeds. In a separate bowl, whisk together the barley and wheatgrass powders with the olive oil and lemon juice. Pour this dressing over the salad, add in the marinated onions and gently toss together. Season and serve.

Chia Seeds are truly a wonder food. They contain 18 of the 22 amino acids including all 9 essential amino acids, making it a 'complete' protein. It is high in fibre and antioxidants, and most importantly it has a 3-to-1 ratio of omega 3s to 6s, making it a very useful addition to any meal.

Tabbouleh salad

Did you know that parsley contains a huge amount of vitamin K, which supports bone strength and protection against Alzheimer's? Parsley is rich in iron and has three times the amount of vitamin C as oranges, too, which is harmonious since iron requires the presence of vitamin C in order to be absorbed by the body. Perfect!

Serves 4-6 as a main dish

1 large head of cauliflower

approx 4-5 tbsp fresh coriander, chopped

approx 5 tbsp fresh mint, chopped

approx 6 tbsp fresh flat leaf parsley, chopped

1 whole cucumber, diced

1 large red onion, finely chopped

1 large red pepper, finely diced

a handful of cashew nuts, chopped finely

2 lemons, juiced

4 tbsp cold pressed extra virgin olive oil

a pinch of Himalayan pink salt and pepper to taste

pomegranate seeds for sprinkling on top

Start by breaking the cauliflower into large florets and chopping the stalk into large pieces (discard any really fibrous bits at the end of the stalk). Pulse the cauliflower in batches in a food processor; you want a fine grainy texture, similar to couscous, not a mush. Transfer the cauliflower 'rice' to a large bowl. Mix all of the other ingredients into the cauliflower, check the seasoning and serve with a sprinkle of pomegranate seeds.

Cauliflower makes a good alternative to rice or couscous in a raw salad but do try other root vegetables; parsnips work well and add an earthy sweetness to the dish.

Tomato & pomegranate

Serves 4-6 as a side dish

———

1 red onion, finely chopped

1 tsp raw, unfiltered apple cider vinegar

1 tsp coconut nectar

1 tsp Himalayan pink salt

approx 500g mixed coloured cherry tomatoes

1 pomegranate, deseeded

¼ - ½ tsp ground allspice

a pinch of Himalayan pink salt and pepper

2 tbsp cold pressed extra virgin olive oil

juice of a lemon

4-5 tbsp fresh, chopped coriander and parsley

a small handful of green olives, stoned (optional)

2 handfuls of washed escarole or purple endive leaves, chopped (optional)

Tomatoes come in a variety of shapes, colours and flavours. Try introducing a variety to liven up this salad, both in taste and vibrancy.

In a small bowl, mix together the chopped red onion, apple cider vinegar, coconut nectar and salt. Massage this mixture with your hands, squeezing the salt into the onions. Once the onions are well combined, cover and leave for at least 15 minutes. Meanwhile, halve the cherry tomatoes over the serving bowl you wish to use and add the pomegranate seeds. In a bowl, whisk together the allspice, salt, pepper, olive oil and lemon juice. Check the taste and add more seasoning if necessary. Stir the dressing through the tomatoes, along with the fresh herbs and red onion. Adjust the seasoning for the last time and serve.

Adding the olives and/or endive will add another level of texture, colour and flavour. The endive leaves also add bulk if you're trying to feed a crowd. Escarole is an exquisite member of the endive family with the same fresh, mildly bitter flavour. It looks like a bright purple curly kale and works really well with the sweetness of the tomatoes and allspice.

Pomegranates are quite the remarkable fruit. They are antioxidant powerhouses and so too is the peel of the fruit. Don't waste the peel, as it can be juiced to release the nutrients! The seeds of pomegranates are rich in fibre, vitamins and minerals and also some bioactive compounds.

Watermelon, strawberry & mint salad Heal

Serves 6

———

1 small watermelon, deseeded
and cut into small chunks

approx 12 fresh strawberries,
sliced

juice of ½ lemon

a pinch of Himalayan pink salt

a pinch of red chilli flakes

a small handful of fresh mint,
roughly chopped

50g feta cheese, crumbled (optional)

This bright, fresh raw salad is perfect on a hot summer's day and takes
minutes to prepare. It is a take on the classic watermelon and feta
salad, but only add the cheese if you're not wanting a raw vegan dish.

Mix all of the ingredients together gently and serve in a large, shallow
bowl with a scatter of mint leaves on top.

———

*Strawberries are not just beautiful to
look at and tasty to eat, but deliver
a range of health-promoting benefits,
such as anti-aging properties, eye
health, easing inflammation, lowering
risk of cardiovascular disease and
boosting short-term memory.
The major thing to be careful of is
the non-organic kind; strawberries
rank among the highest for chemical
residue on conventional produce.*

Maintain

~

This is our mezzo chapter of recipes! We love these dishes because they are healthy but are packed full of taste, colour and texture, and will satiate anyone. They use less of the decadent ingredients that many people are trying to cut down on, without sacrificing flavour.

The dishes combine healthy foods with less of an emphasis on meats, heavy creams and refined starch, without compromising on taste and wow factor. These are great dishes to help introduce your family to slightly healthier options that don't make anyone feel like they're missing out on the indulgences they might be used to.

Asparagus with herb oil

Serves 4 as a side dish

a little coconut oil

8-12 vine-ripened, cherry tomatoes

18 asparagus spears

FOR THE HERB OIL:

a small handful each of fresh
chives, basil and flat leaf parsley

2 tbsp capers, drained

juice of ½ lemon

a pinch of Himalayan pink salt and
freshly ground black pepper

approx 8 tbsp cold pressed extra
virgin olive oil

extra Himalayan pink salt and freshly
ground black pepper to season

1 tbsp nigella seeds

2-3 tbsp capers, drained (optional)

Preheat the oven to 200°C / 400°F / Gas Mark 6.

Rub a little coconut oil over the surface of a shallow baking tray and lay out the cherry tomatoes; leave them on the vine, if possible. Roast the tomatoes for approximately 20 minutes, or until soft and lightly charred. Meanwhile, prep the asparagus by snapping off any fibrous ends and cut any thick spears in half, lengthwise. Heat a griddle pan over a high heat and melt a little coconut oil. Turn down the heat and griddle the asparagus in batches until ridged brown but not too soft. Drain the cooked asparagus on some kitchen paper and set aside.

To make the herb oil, simply blend all the ingredients together in a food processor and season. The herb oil can be made in advance but will lose some of its vibrant green colour.

Serve the charred asparagus and tomatoes on a large platter, drizzled with the herb oil and scatter over the nigella seeds and some extra capers, if you like.

Capers may seem a little insignificant, but these little buds relieve rheumatic pain, are analgesic and antibacterial and also have some anticarcinogenic properties too! They are fibre rich and also have the power to neutralise certain byproducts from bad food sources containing high fat content.

Asparagus with quail's eggs

Serves 4 as a side dish

———

12 quail's eggs

18 asparagus spears

cashew nut cheese (see page 20)

1 tbsp fresh chives, finely chopped

1 tbsp fresh coriander, finely chopped

a pinch of Himalayan pink salt and freshly ground black pepper

2 tbsp cold pressed extra virgin olive oil

extra Himalayan pink salt and freshly ground black pepper to season

Bring a medium-sized pan of water up to the boil and boil the quail's eggs for approximately 3 minutes, remove them with a slotted spoon and set aside to cool. While the eggs are cooking, prep the asparagus by snapping off any fibrous ends. Once the eggs have been removed from the water, quickly blanch the asparagus spears for 2-3 minutes in boiling water. The spears should be just cooked and maintain some bite, so the thinner the spears the quicker they will take. Cut any thick spears in half, lengthwise. Drain the cooked asparagus and immediately plunge into cold water to halt the cooking process.

Mix together the cashew nut cheese, herbs, salt and pepper and oil, then toss through the well-drained asparagus. Season to taste and set aside.

Peel the quail's eggs and cut in half. Pile the asparagus onto a platter, top with the egg, scatter over some extra herbs and serve.

This dish can easily adapted to be vegan by simply omitting the quail's eggs from the ingredients.

Avial

Sweet potatoes pack a huge punch of vitamins and minerals and in large quantities! In just one cup of sweet potato, over 200% of the recommended daily amount of vitamin A is present! Vitamins C, B1, B2, B3 and B6 are also found in abundance, and there's no shortage of fibre as well. Sweet potatoes are lighter in starch and better for you than regular potatoes, and they are very versatile in dishes.

Serves 6-8

FOR THE PASTE:

180g chopped fresh or frozen coconut or 120g desiccated (shredded) coconut

1 small onion, chopped

2cm (1") fresh ginger, chopped

4 cloves garlic, crushed

2 chillies, finely chopped

2 tsp turmeric

FOR THE AVIAL:

a mixture of vegetables: carrots, sweet potatoes, squash, green beans, peas etc

a little coconut oil

1 tsp each of coriander and cumin seeds

half a cabbage, thinly sliced

a handful of fresh coriander, chopped

This is a take on a classic dish from Kerala in southern India. The best way to describe it is an Indian stir-fry - a fresher, drier dish than a traditional curry and, once the paste is made, a very quick and easy dish to produce.

Blitz together all the ingredients in a food processor until smooth. Store in an airtight container in the fridge.

Start by peeling and prepping the vegetables. Baton or slice the carrots and cut the sweet potatoes into small batons or chunks etc. Then steam or blanch each of the vegetables until al dente; the time this takes will depend on the density and size of the vegetables. To save on using lots of pans, just start with the harder root vegetables (carrots, potatoes) and add in the softer greens after a few minutes. Drain and cool in ice cold water; this can be done a day before to save on time.

When ready to cook, melt the coconut oil on a medium heat in a heavy-based pan. Quickly fry off the seeds and then add the Avial paste, roughly 1 tablespoon per person. Stir-fry the paste for a few minutes, then add the cabbage. Toss the cabbage through the spices to soak up the flavours then add all the other vegetables. Stir-fry until heated through. Then toss in the fresh herbs, season with salt and pepper and serve.

Any leftover paste can be stored in the fridge for at least a week, or freeze.

Traditionally, paprika has been used in the East for so many health-promoting benefits, as well as for its flavour in food preparation. It aids digestion by normalising the acid in the stomach and it promotes restful sleep, as it contributes to the production of the 'sleep hormone', melatonin. Paprika also contains anti-aging properties such as beta-carotene.

Basic hummus

Serves 4-6

———

100g raw chickpeas

juice of a lemon

3 cloves garlic, peeled

1 tsp ground cumin

1 tsp sweet paprika

4 tbsp tahini (sesame seed paste) (optional)

6 tbsp cold pressed extra virgin olive oil

Himalayan pink salt and pepper to taste

Start by soaking the chickpeas in plenty of cold water overnight. It is possible to cook from raw, but it takes about 2 hours. When ready to make the hummus, drain the chickpeas and rinse well. Boil the chickpeas in plenty of water until tender, approximately 30-40 minutes. When they are cooked, drain and rinse in plenty of cold water. Tip all the ingredients into a food processor and blitz until smooth. The texture is very dependent on personal taste; make it as coarse or smooth as you like, even reserve some whole chickpeas to mix in at the end. Season the hummus and add a little more olive oil if too dry. Serve with raw vegetables or use to top a baked potato.

Try adding other ingredients to vary the flavours - fresh herbs, spring onion and roasted peppers work well. At the restaurant we do a great dish of roasted sweet potato with burnt aubergine hummus; use the recipe above and blend in a whole charred and roasted aubergine.

Beetroot & cumin falafels

**Makes 10-12 medium
or 24-26 small falafels**

———

approx 4 tbsp coconut oil

1 tsp each of cumin seeds and
coriander seeds

2 cardamom pods

1 medium onion, finely chopped

1cm (½") chunk ginger, grated

2 cloves garlic, crushed

1 tsp cayenne pepper

2-3 medium beetroot bulbs, washed
and cleaned

a handful of chives and coriander,
chopped

approx 100g gram (chickpea) flour

a little rice or almond milk

Himalayan pink salt and pepper

extra coconut oil, for frying

Preheat the oven to 200°C / 400°F / Gas Mark 6.

Heat the coconut oil in a heavy-based frying pan on a medium heat. Add the cumin and coriander seeds and fry for a few minutes to release the flavours (do not burn; they will taste bitter). Meanwhile, crush the cardamom pods, scrape out the seeds and add to the pan. Now throw in the onion, ginger, garlic and cayenne pepper and continue to fry until soft (add a little water occasionally to stop anything from burning). While the onion is cooking, either grate the beetroot with a coarse grater, or chop into large pieces and pulse in a food processor (the finer pieces work better when making canapé-sized falafels, but it is a personal choice). Squeeze out any excess liquid and add the beetroot to the pan. Continue to fry until the beetroot begins to soften a little, about 5 minutes. Take off the heat and stir through the fresh herbs. Taste and season with salt and pepper. At this stage the mixture should be quite dry, so drain off any excess liquid. Now sieve in the gram flour and stir through the falafel mix, beating in any lumps of flour. Leave the mixture to stand for about 5 minutes to allow the flour to bind with the vegetables. If the mixture is too dry, stir through a little rice or almond milk. The mixture should bind together and you should be able to mould small patties in your hands. If the mixture is excessively wet or dry this will be very hard to do, so adjust the texture by adding a little more flour and/or milk.

Wipe clean the frying pan and heat up a good 2-3mm coconut oil. Mould your patties and drop into the hot oil. Fry for a few minutes before attempting to move them. Once they have crisped up on the underside they should be easy to lift with a thin fish slice and flip over. Once they are brown on each side, they should be ready to eat, but if they are quite thick, continue cooking on a baking sheet in the oven for a further 10 minutes. It is possible to drain the falafel on kitchen paper, once fried, and reserve for later; either leave them on the side and reheat in a hot oven for 10 minutes, or refrigerate for 2-3 days and reheat when needed.

Coriander seeds are seen as one of the more healing herb seeds. They are phytonutrient dense, which means they contain many naturally occurring plant chemicals that protect the plant from germs, fungi and other pathogens. When we eat phytonutrients, our bodies receive the same benefits and protection that the plants do from having them as part of their composition.

Raw coconut nectar is the sap from the coconut blossom. Its taste is sweet and much like maple syrup, only it is raw and thus has had its nutritional profile both unaffected and unadulterated by processing. It contains 17 of 22 amino acids, including all the essential ones, and is rich in minerals, vitamins and has beneficial live enzymes. It is also low on the glycaemic index.

Capers   DF GF,

a   GF, DF

V, GF,

GF

contain egg, DF

choke Hearts

Cannellini beans with chilli & fresh herbs

Serves 6 as a side dish

———

400g dried cannellini beans, soaked overnight in plenty of cold water.

FOR THE CHILLI SAUCE:

6 cloves garlic, peeled

2cm (1") chunk of fresh ginger

4-5 red chillies, deseeded - adjust the number of chillies depending on how hot you like it!

3 tbsp fresh lemon juice

approx 60g coconut nectar

a little raw, unfiltered apple cider vinegar

FOR THE SALAD:

3 bell peppers, deseeded and coarsely chopped

4 spring onions, chopped

a small handful of coriander and mint, chopped

2 tbsp nigella seeds

2 radishes, thinly sliced

Start by cooking the beans in plenty of water. Bring to the boil, removing the scum off the surface at regular intervals. After about 10 minutes, reduce the heat, cover and simmer for an hour or so - the beans should be soft but not breaking up. Do not add any salt, as this will toughen the skin.

While the beans are cooking, make your chilli sauce. Blitz all the ingredients in a food processor. Scrape the sauce into a small pan and heat gently. Cook for 5 minutes. Taste and adjust the flavours by adding more lemon juice, vinegar and coconut nectar, until it is to your liking. The end result should be hot, sweet and sour. The sauce is quite fiery, but you can adjust how much you add to the salad using a little organic, cold pressed extra virgin olive oil and lemon juice to create a less spicy dressing than just the chilli sauce alone.

Once the beans are cooked, rinse them in plenty of cold water and place in a large bowl. Add the chopped peppers, spring onions, herbs and nigella seeds, then stir through enough chilli sauce to coat the beans. Taste and adjust the seasoning and serve decorated with the radish. This dish also works well hot as a vegan main.

Caraway & mustard seed spiced cabbage with celery & currants

Serves 4-6 as a side dish

———

2 tbsp coconut oil

6-8 shallots, finely sliced

1 tsp caraway seeds

1 tsp mustard seeds

8 curry leaves

2 tbsp fresh thyme, chopped

1 tbsp za'atar*

a small white cabbage, thinly shredded

4 sticks of celery, thinly sliced

70-80g currants

a small handful fresh of oregano, chopped

2 tbsp pine nuts

Himalayan pink salt and pepper

*Za'atar is a herb and spice mix used in many Middle Eastern dishes. It's easy to make your own:
6 tablespoons of sumac, 1 tbsp Himalayan pink salt and 2 tbsp each of dried thyme, oregano, marjoram and toasted sesame seeds.
Mix all together and store!

Heat the oil in a large, heavy-based frying pan over a medium heat and add the onions. Sauté for about 5 minutes until light brown. Add the caraway seeds, mustard seeds, curry leaves, thyme, za'atar and a little salt and pepper. Continue stir frying for 2-3 minutes and then add in the shredded cabbage.

Continue frying until the cabbage begins to soften, pouring in a little water every few minutes to stop the cabbage from burning onto the pan. Once the cabbage is cooked, spoon the contents of the pan into a large mixing bowl.

Allow the mixture to cool a little and then add the celery, currants and oregano. Check the seasoning and add salt and pepper, if needed. Scatter over the pine nuts and serve.

———

ORAC is the ranking system that measures the ability of any given food to absorb oxygen, which is good for our cells. Currants have a high ORAC value, which means that they are fabulous little antioxidant powerhouses. They carry significantly high levels of phenolic flavonoid phytochemicals called anthocyanins, which studies have shown can have potential health effects against aging, some neurological diseases and even cancer.

Carrot & harissa salad

Cloves rank among the very top on the ORAC scale (Oxygen Radical Absorbance Capacity), making them supreme antioxidants. They have been used for centuries in natural healing for their antibacterial, antiseptic and antifungal properties. They increase circulation, boost the immune system, are a good treatment for indigestion and are also anti-inflammatory.

Serves 6 as a side dish

6 large carrots, peeled and cut into thin diagonal slices (a mandolin is best to get thin, even slices)

2 tbsp coconut oil

1 tsp caraway seeds

1 tsp cumin seeds

1 tsp ground cinnamon

a pinch of ground cloves

1 large red onion, thinly sliced

2 cloves garlic, crushed

2 tbsp harissa paste (see page 108)

juice and zest of an unwaxed orange

Himalayan pink salt and pepper

a little extra fresh lemon juice

TO FINISH THE SALAD:

1 small red onion, thinly sliced

1 tbsp coconut nectar

1 tbsp raw, unfiltered apple cider vinegar

a cup of boiling water

a little Himalayan pink salt

approx 3-4 large handfuls of rocket leaves

Cook the carrots in plenty of water. They need to be al dente, and the cooking time will depend on the thickness of the slices, so watch carefully. Once cooked, drain and refresh in cold water to stop the cooking process.

When ready to make the salad, heat the coconut oil in a heavy-based frying pan and toast the seeds, followed by the ground spices. Now add the onion and garlic and continue to fry until caramelised and soft. Stir in the harissa paste, orange zest and juice, followed by the carrots. Taste and season; it may need a little lemon juice to add acidity.

While the onions and spices are frying, tip the thinly sliced red onion into a small bowl, add the coconut nectar, vinegar and salt and massage into the onion with your hands. Cover in boiling water and leave for a few minutes. Once the carrot and onion mix is ready, tip into a large serving bowl and gently toss through the rocket leaves. Drain and squeeze any water from the red onions, scatter over the salad and serve.

Carrot & sesame seed falafels

Step aside vitamin A pills, the carrot is here - and always has been! Carrots, with their enormous amounts of beta-carotene, will improve eyesight, reduce macular degeneration, prevent cancer and improve digestive health all-round. They reduce risk of heart attack and alleviate high blood pressure because they dilate blood vessels.

Makes 10-12 medium or 24-26 small falafels

approx 4 tbsp coconut oil

1 tsp each of cumin seeds and coriander seeds

2 cardamom pods

1 medium onion, finely chopped

1cm (½") chunk of ginger, grated

2 cloves garlic, crushed

½ tsp crushed chilli flakes

5-6 medium carrots, washed and cleaned

a handful of spring onions, chopped

3 tbsp sesame seeds

approx 100g gram (chickpea) flour

a little rice or almond milk

Himalayan pink salt and pepper to taste

extra coconut oil, for frying

Preheat the oven to 200°C / 400°F / Gas Mark 6.

Heat the coconut oil in a heavy-based frying pan on a medium heat. Add the cumin and coriander seeds and fry for a few minutes to release the flavours (do not burn; they will taste bitter). Meanwhile, crush the cardamom pods, scrape out the seeds and add to the pan. Now throw in the onion, ginger, garlic and chilli flakes and continue to fry until soft (add a little water occasionally to stop anything from burning). While the onion is cooking, either grate the carrots with a coarse grater, or chop into large pieces and pulse in a food processor (the finer pieces work better when making canapé-sized falafels, but it is a personal choice). Squeeze out any excess liquid and add the carrots to the pan. Continue to fry until the carrot begins to soften a little, about 5-10 minutes. Take off the heat and stir through the spring onion and sesame seeds. Taste and season with salt and pepper. At this stage the mixture should be quite dry, so drain off any excess liquid. Now sieve in the gram flour and stir through the falafel mix, beating in any lumps of flour. Leave the mixture to stand for about 5 minutes to allow the flour to bind with the vegetables. If the mixture is too dry, stir through a little rice or almond milk. The mixture should bind together so you are able to mould small patties in your hands. If the mixture is excessively wet or dry, this will be very hard to do, so adjust the texture by adding a little more flour and/or milk.

Wipe clean the frying pan and heat up a good 2-3mm of coconut oil. Mould your patties and drop into the hot oil. Fry for a few minutes before attempting to move them. Once they have crisped up on the underside, they should be easy to lift with a thin fish slice and flip over. Once they are brown on each side they should be ready to eat, but if they are quite thick, continue cooking on a baking sheet in the oven for a further 10 minutes. It is possible to drain the falafel on kitchen paper, once fried, and reserve for later; either leave them on the side and reheat in a hot oven for 10 minutes, or refrigerate for 2-3 days and reheat when needed.

Celeriac with puy lentils & thyme

Serves 4-6 as a side dish

———

approx 200g puy lentils

2 bay leaves

4-6 sprigs of fresh thyme (save the soft tender tips to garnish)

1 small to medium celeriac, cut into thin chips (a mandolin is great for this)

juice of a lemon

4-6 tbsp cold pressed extra virgin olive oil

3-4 tbsp raw, unfiltered apple cider vinegar

a small handful flat leaf parsley, chopped

2-3 tbsp fresh thyme, finely chopped (use the reserved tips)

1 tsp sweet paprika

Himalayan pink salt and pepper to taste

Cook the lentils in a large pan of water with the bay leaves and thyme sprigs. Bring to the boil and simmer for approximately 15 minutes until cooked but still al dente. Drain off through a sieve.

Meanwhile, cook the celeriac by dropping into a pan of boiling water with half the lemon juice. Depending on how thin your strips are, this could take from 1-3 minutes; they need to be tender but still firm. Drain the celeriac and reserve.

In a large serving bowl, mix the warm lentils with the oil, vinegar, salt and pepper. Stir through the fresh herbs, paprika and cooked celeriac then adjust the seasoning (add the remaining lemon juice if you like). This dish is best served warm and makes a great vegan main dish as well as an accompaniment. Add some extra texture with a handful of toasted nuts and/or seeds.

———

Celeriac is the bulb out of which the head of celery grows. Despite not being as universally recognised, it is nevertheless quite the powerhouse of nutrients as it helps cure kidney diseases, activates the metabolism for aiding weight loss, improves skin and hair condition, relaxes nerves and regulates bowel movements. It is surprisingly versatile and can be used in juices as well as meals.

Chickpea & tomato stew

*Chickpeas are very high in fibre, which aids in the reduction
of hypotension and protects against heart disease through the
lowering of bad cholesterol. It has an alkalising effect on the body
and also is a source of many of the key minerals such as iron,
zinc, folate and phosphorus.*

Serves 6 as a main dish

200g raw chickpeas

a little coconut oil

1 tsp coriander seeds

1 tsp cumin seeds

1 tsp smoked paprika

2 onions, sliced

3 cloves garlic, crushed

1cm (½") chunk fresh ginger, grated

1 jar passata (sieved tomatoes)

Himalayan pink salt and pepper
to taste

Start by soaking the chickpeas in plenty of cold water overnight. It is possible to cook from raw, but it takes about 2 hours. When ready to make the stew, drain the chickpeas and rinse well. Boil the chickpeas in plenty of water until tender, approximately 30-40 minutes. When they are cooked, drain and rinse in plenty of cold water.

While the chickpeas are cooking, heat up the coconut oil in a deep, heavy-based pan on a medium heat. Fry the coriander and cumin seeds for a few minutes to release their aromas - do not burn! Add in the paprika, onion, garlic and ginger and fry until the onion softens. Add a little water if they begin to stick to the pan. Pour in the tomatoes and stir through the chickpeas. Bring the pan up to the boil then lower the heat and cover. Simmer the stew for about 20 minutes to infuse the flavours. Serve with steamed rice or mop up with homemade chapatis.

Chickpeas with mangetout & roasted tomatoes

Mangetout is actually a nutrient-dense vegetable, even though it seems quite unassuming. It is great for heart health, for fighting infections and is great for hair and skin as well. It also is good for reducing cognitive decline because of its neurological boosting properties.

Serves 6 as a main dish

200g raw chickpeas

a little coconut oil, for roasting and frying

approx 18 small, vine-ripened tomatoes, ideally still on the vine

a sprig of fresh rosemary

4 bay leaves

approx 200g fresh mangetout, topped and tailed if necessary

1 tsp coriander seeds

1 tsp ajwain seeds

1 tsp sweet paprika

1 onion, finely diced

3 cloves garlic, crushed

1cm (½") chunk fresh ginger, grated

Himalayan pink salt and pepper to taste

Set the oven to 200°C / 400°F / Gas Mark 6.

Start by soaking the chickpeas in plenty of cold water overnight. It is possible to cook from raw, but it takes about 2 hours. When ready to make the dish, drain the chickpeas and rinse well. Boil the chickpeas in plenty of water until tender, approximately 30-40 minutes. When they are cooked, drain and rinse in plenty of cold water.

While the chickpeas are cooking, rub a little coconut oil over a small, flat roasting tin. Lay on the rosemary and bay leaves, followed by the tomatoes. Slide the tin into the centre of the oven and roast until soft but still holding their shape, approximately 30 minutes. Once cooked, remove the stalks and set aside.

Boil a large pan of water and cook the mangetout for a few minutes only (you want them to retain their freshness and bite). Immediately plunge the cooked beans into cold water to halt the cooking process. Drain and reserve for later.

Heat up a few tablespoons of coconut oil in a deep, heavy-based frying pan on a medium heat. Fry off the coriander and ajwain seeds for a few minutes to release their aromas - do not burn! Add in the paprika, onion, garlic and ginger and fry until the onion softens. Add a little water if they begin to stick to the pan. Pour in the chickpeas and continue to fry for about 5 minutes, so they can absorb some of the flavours. Finally, add in the roasted tomatoes and stir through the mangetout. Stir-fry the whole dish for a few minutes to combine all the ingredients, season and serve.

Coconut & curry leaf soup with chickpea dumplings

Serves 4-6

———

FOR THE SOUP:

4-6 tbsp coconut oil

1 tbsp black mustard seeds

2cm (1") chunk of fresh ginger, chopped

6-8 curry leaves

1 dried red chilli

4 tbsp gram (chickpea) flour

120ml coconut cream or natural set yogurt

240ml coconut milk

120ml filtered water

1 small handful of coriander stalks, finely chopped (keep the leaves for garnishing)

FOR THE DUMPLINGS:

120g gram (chickpea) flour

1 tsp cumin seeds

½ tsp turmeric

2 tbsp fresh coriander, chopped

a pinch of Himalayan pink salt and black pepper

a pinch of gluten-free baking powder

1 small onion, finely diced

¼ tsp red chilli flakes (optional)

coconut oil for shallow frying

For the soup

Heat the coconut oil in a large, deep pan. Add the mustard seeds and, as they start crackling, add the ginger, curry leaves and the red chilli. Fry gently for 2-3 minutes. While the spices are cooking, tip the gram flour into a bowl and slowly beat in the coconut cream or yogurt to form a smooth paste. Now stir in the coconut milk and add this mixture to the pan of spices. Bring the pan to the boil, add coriander stalks, then turn the heat down and simmer for 8-10 minutes. The gram flour will interact with the milk to thicken the soup. So increase the heat to a more rapid boil if the soup is too thin; you are looking for a smooth, creamy texture. When the soup is done, season and serve, garnished with fresh coriander.

For the dumplings

Mix all of the ingredients together, adding enough water to turn it into a thick paste. Heat the coconut oil in a small frying pan. Drop about a tablespoon of the batter into the oil and cook until golden brown. Do not make the dumplings too big as they may not cook through; check the first one by tearing in half and eating it! Drain the fried dumplings on kitchen paper and serve the soup with the dumplings on the side.

Curry leaves don't just add the distinctive flavour we are all familiar with; they have many medicinal properties too. Such as the ability to lower blood sugar levels, regulate the digestive system and prevent anaemia - as they are a rich source of iron. They relieve indigestion and improve a damaged liver due to their content of kaempferol - a potent antioxidant.

Eliane potato salad

Serves 8 as a side dish

_____

FOR THE CASHEW NUT MAYONNAISE:

100g raw cashew nuts

1 tbsp mustard

1-2 tsp raw, unfiltered apple
cider vinegar

4-6 tbsp cold pressed extra virgin
olive oil

1 tsp each of Himalayan pink salt
and black pepper

approx 70ml freshly squeezed
apple juice

FOR THE POTATO SALAD:

1kg of new potatoes

a handful of fresh mint

a handful of fresh coriander

3-4 garlic cloves, peeled

6 tbsp cold pressed extra virgin
olive oil

2 tsp raw, unfiltered apple
cider vinegar

approx 150g fresh (or defrosted from
frozen) peas

Himalayan pink salt and pepper
to taste

a small handful of fresh flat leaf
parsley, chopped

2-3 spring onions, chopped

approx 5 tbsp pine nuts

3 free-range hard-boiled eggs,
halved (optional)

This is a dairy-free version of a classic salad. Everyone in the restaurant loves this and very few people can tell it does not contain traditional mayonnaise!

Start by making the cashew nut mayonnaise. Soak the nuts in plenty of cold water for at least 2 hours. Drain the nuts and blend with all the ingredients, except the apple juice. Once the mixture is smooth, add enough apple juice to create a thick and creamy mayonnaise. Check the seasoning and set aside.

Meanwhile, boil the potatoes until soft but not falling apart, about 10-15 minutes. Drain the potatoes and set aside.

Make a pesto by blending the mint, coriander, garlic cloves, vinegar and half the oil in a blender. Check the seasoning and add a little more oil, if necessary.

Ideally, cut the potatoes in half whilst still warm. To the potatoes add the peas, half the nut mayonnaise and half the pesto. Stir everything together and add more mayonnaise and pesto, if needed. Any leftovers can be stored in the fridge for at least 2-3 days and used to liven up salads or sauces. Add salt and pepper to taste and serve garnished with herbs, spring onion and pine nuts. For added luxury add some hard-boiled eggs. Remember to serve them on the side if you want to make this salad vegan friendly.

French beans with mustard & tarragon

Serves 6 as a side dish

———

600g French beans, tailed (also try using a mixture of mangetout and runner beans)

300g peas (fresh or frozen)

1 clove garlic, peeled

zest and juice of an unwaxed lemon

approx 60ml cold pressed extra virgin olive oil

2 tsp sesame seeds

1 tsp nigella seeds

½ tsp of crushed, dried chilli

4-5 tbsp fresh tarragon, chopped

Himalayan pink salt and pepper to taste

Bring a large pan of water to the boil and blanch the beans for 2-3 minutes. Lift out with a sieve and immediately plunge into cold water. Repeat with the peas but only cook for a minute. Drain off the refreshed greens, dry and place into a large serving bowl.

In a mortar, pound the garlic clove with some salt and mix in the zest and juice of the lemon and some of the olive oil. In a small, pan dry-fry the sesame seeds until lightly toasted. Pour the contents of the pan over the beans, followed by the garlic and lemon dressing; stir through the dish and season to taste. Scatter over the nigella seeds, chilli and tarragon. Give the salad one final toss and serve. This dish also works well hot and is lovely with roasted chicken for a lazy weekend lunch.

For a larger salad add some salad leaves; rocket is a perfect choice as it holds its shape and texture, while some of the softer leaves will wilt more easily when the dressing is added.

Tarragon has been used in various traditional medicines for centuries for stimulating the appetite and as a remedy for anorexia, flatulence and hiccups. Laboratory studies on tarragon proved certain compounds contained therein inhibit platelet activation, resulting in the prevention of platelet aggregation and adhesion to the blood vessel wall. What this means is that tarragon can help prevent clot formation inside tiny blood vessels of the heart and brain which protect from heart attack and stroke.

Gajar Mata Sabzi
(pea & carrot curry with coconut)

Serves 6 as a side dish

———

2 tbsp coconut oil

1 tsp each of coriander and cumin seeds

1 tsp mustard seeds

¼ tsp turmeric

½ tsp garam masala

1cm (½") chunk of ginger, finely grated

1 chilli, deseeded and finely chopped

8 curry leaves

4 large carrots, peeled and diced

200g fresh or frozen peas

Himalayan pink salt and pepper to taste

a small handful of coconut chips, or a sprinkling of desiccated coconut to serve

Start by heating the coconut oil in a heavy-based deep frying pan over a medium heat. Tip in the coriander and cumin seeds and fry for a minute to release their aromas - be careful not to burn. Next add the mustard seeds, turmeric, garam masala, ginger, chilli and curry leaves. Continue to fry for a few minutes, adding a little water to stop the spices sticking to the pan. Next add the carrots and a little water and fry until the carrots just begin to soften. Tip in the peas and stir-fry for a few more minutes (a little longer if the peas are still frozen). Season and serve scattered with coconut.

———

Don't shy away from using spices in your dishes. Garam masala is not actually an individual spice but a combination of spices that almost everyone is familiar with in one way or another. Ayurvedics traditionally combined cumin, fennel seed, coriander seed, bay leaf and black pepper to create garam masala. The flavours are magnificent together, and they combine all their respective health promoting benefits too.

Swiss chard is very nutrient dense with exceptionally high levels of vitamins K, A and C. Try this recipe with fresh beet leaves, which add a beautiful purple hue. A great way to get everyone to eat their greens!

Green beans with chard & feta

Serves 4-6 as a side dish

400g French beans, tailed (also try
using a mixture of mangetout and
runner beans)

2 tbsp coconut oil

a large bunch of chard leaves, torn
and stems roughly chopped

2 cloves garlic, peeled

zest and juice of a small
unwaxed lemon

approx 60ml cold pressed extra
virgin olive oil

approx 3cm (1 ½") block of feta
cheese

Himalayan pink salt and pepper
to taste

Bring a large pan of water to the boil and blanch the beans for 3-4
minutes. Lift out with a sieve and immediately plunge into cold water.
Drain off the refreshed greens, dry and place into a large serving bowl.
Heat the coconut oil in a large, heavy-based frying pan and flash-fry the
chard for a few minutes. Add the lightly stir-fried chard to the green beans.

In a mortar, pound the garlic with some salt, mix in the zest and juice
of the lemon and add the oil. Pour the garlicky lemon mixture over the
beans and chard, stir through the dish and season to taste. Arrange the
greens on a large platter, crumble over the feta and serve.

Griddled asparagus & samphire

Serves 4-6 as a side dish

approx 24 asparagus spears

2-3 tbsp coconut oil

150g samphire, washed

1 clove garlic, crushed

squeeze of fresh lemon juice

4-5 tbsp cold pressed extra virgin olive oil

1 small handful each of fresh flat leaf parsley and dill, chopped

1 tsp of cracked black pepper

1 tsp sesame seeds (optional)

4-6 radishes, thinly sliced

Trim the asparagus by removing the fibrous ends (usually the spear will snap at the point that it becomes tough). Any thicker spears should be cut in half lengthwise. Heat up a ridged griddle pan until searing hot. Add a little coconut oil and griddle off the spears in batches. Place the charred spears into a large serving bowl. Lastly, turn down the heat a bit and fry off the samphire for a few minutes in a little coconut oil (the same pan is fine). Mix all the remaining ingredients together to make a dressing and toss through the salad. Season, sprinkle with sesame seeds and radish slices and serve. Remember that the samphire adds a deep saltiness to the salad, so only add extra salt once you have tasted it.

To make a larger salad for a crowd, finish the dish as above and then gently toss through some leaves, watercress, rocket, spinach etc. Also, some cooked French beans, along with the asparagus, will make this salad go a bit further! Add a little more oil and lemon juice, if necessary. Season and serve. This salad looks lovely sprinkled with sesame seeds. Also try black onion or nigella seeds (there are a lot of differing opinions as to whether black onion seeds and nigella seeds are the same thing. For the sake of this salad, let's say they are!).

Samphire is a wonderfully versatile sea vegetable that is deliciously salty but equally abundant in benefits. It is a rich source of vitamins A, B and C and is also a source of folic acid. It improves visual clarity, mental alertness, concentration and muscle function. It eases kidney complaints and cleanses the liver too. Samphire goes well in so many dishes, it's a shame to not make the most of this incredible plant food.

Griddled aubergine with herb oil

Chives are beautifully balanced in terms of flavour, texture and nutritional benefits. They are members of the Allium genus family, which includes onion and garlic, so they don't just make a pretty garnish! They have been shown to have cancer prevention activity, immune system boosting stimulators, heart-health compounds and bone-health minerals.

Serves 4

FOR THE HERB OIL:

2 handfuls of soft herbs: flat leaf parsley, chives, coriander, basil etc

2-3 tbsp capers

approx 60ml cold pressed extra virgin olive oil

Himalayan pink salt and pepper

2 large aubergines, sliced lengthwise into medium-thick slices (approx 3-4 mm)

a little coconut oil

Blend the herbs, capers, oil, salt and pepper together in a food processor, taste and adjust seasoning. The oil can be kept in the fridge for up to a week but will lose its vibrant colour.

Heat a large ridged griddle pan over a high heat. Add the coconut oil and allow it to melt. Char the aubergines on either side in batches and keep warm on a covered plate. Arrange the aubergine on a large platter, sprinkle with salt and pepper and dollop on the herb oil.

Griddled cauliflower with herbs, tomatoes & capers

Of the phytonutrients available in grapes, the one that has been linked to longevity is resveratrol. Resveratrol is the reason you hear people say that drinking red wine every day is good for the heart, but the truth is you do not need the added alcohol when you can obtain the active ingredient directly from the fresh fruit itself!

Serves 4-6 as a side dish

1 small cauliflower separated into florets

FOR THE DRESSING:

2 tsp drained capers

4 garlic cloves, crushed

2 tsp raw, unfiltered apple cider vinegar

60-70ml cold pressed extra virgin olive oil

1 tbsp wholegrain mustard

a pinch of Himalayan pink salt and black pepper

TO FINISH THE SALAD:

180g halved, black seedless grapes

approx 10-15 cherry tomatoes, halved

a small handful each of fresh flat leaf parsley, dill and mint, chopped

Set oven to 200°C / 400°F / Gas Mark 6.

Blanch the cauliflower in boiling salted water for approximately 3 minutes, until cooked but still with some bite. Drain the florets and plunge into cold water to stop the cooking process.

While the cauliflower is cooking, make the dressing by whisking together the capers, garlic, vinegar and mustard. Continue whisking while slowly pouring in the olive oil to form a slightly creamy dressing. Season with salt and pepper and set aside.

Heat a large griddle pan over a high heat. While the pan is getting to temperature, slice the cauliflower florets in half to expose a flat surface. Griddle the cauliflower on the flat side until slightly charred by the ridged pan.

Toss together the griddled cauliflower with the grapes, tomatoes and herbs in a large serving bowl. Pour over enough of the dressing to coat all the ingredients and serve.

When cooking for a crowd, it is simpler to roast the cauliflower in a large tin to save on time. Smear the roasting tin with a little coconut oil and roast the florets for approximately 30 minutes, or until slightly soft and a little charred.

"Let food be thy medicine and medicine be thy food."
Hippocrates

Harissa paste

Caraway is best known as the crunchy seed that gives rye bread its distinctive look and scent, but this flavoursome kitchen spice is a good remedy for colds and congestion. It contains mild antihistamines and antimicrobial compounds that help to relax the muscles that cause coughing spasms. It is also one of the best herbs to prevent gas and bloating. Caraway seeds are also used in a number of medicinal preparations for treating toothaches, eye infections and conditions such as rheumatism.

Makes approximately 200ml

1-2 red peppers

a little coconut oil

1 tsp coriander seeds

½ tsp cumin and caraway seeds

1 small red onion, chopped

4 cloves garlic, crushed

2-3 hot, red chillies, finely chopped (remove the seeds if you want to reduce the heat)

3-4 tbsp tomato purée, or 5-6 sundried tomatoes

juice of half a lemon

1 tsp Himalayan pink salt

Set the oven to 220°C / 440°F / Gas Mark 7-8.

Start by roasting the peppers in a hot oven until the skin is blackened and begins to peel. Alternatively, this can be done under a hot grill; just keep an eye on them. Place the cooked peppers in a large bowl and cover with cling film. Set the bowl to one side until cool. Once cool, the flesh will have begun to shrink away from the skin, allowing the peel to be removed easily.

While the peppers are roasting, heat a small, heavy-based frying pan and dry-fry the spices for a few minutes, being careful not to let them burn. Now add a little coconut oil, followed by the onions, garlic and chillies, and continue to cook until soft and very caramelised.

As everything is frying, peel and deseed the cooled peppers and pop the flesh into a food processor. Add the fried onion mix along with the tomato, lemon and salt. Blitz everything together to form a smooth paste. The paste can be stored in the fridge for about 2 weeks and freezes well.

Herb stuffed potato cakes

Serves 6 as a main dish

———

approx 1kg waxy potatoes
(Maris Piper are great)

1 tbsp mustard seeds

1 tsp ground turmeric

1 tsp cumin seeds, toasted

Himalayan pink salt and pepper

a small handful each of fresh
coriander, mint and flat leaf parsley

3 cloves of garlic, peeled

1cm (½") cube of fresh ginger

2 green chillies, roughly chopped
(deseed and/or reduce the number
to add less heat)

2 tbsp tamarind paste

2 tbsp gram (chickpea) flour

3 tbsp rice flour

approx 80g flaked almonds

coconut oil, for frying

Set oven to 200°C / 400°F / Gas Mark 6.

First, peel and chop the potatoes and cook in plenty of salted water
until soft. Drain well and mash with a little coconut oil, the mustard
seeds, turmeric, toasted cumin seeds and a little salt and pepper.

Place the fresh herbs, garlic, ginger, chillies and tamarind into a food
processor and blitz until it forms a smooth, firm paste. Taste and adjust
the seasoning, if necessary.

Mix together the flours and pile onto a clean work surface. Take a
spoonful of potato, make a dent in the centre, add a small dollop of
the herb mix and roll into a ball, encasing the mixture into the centre of
the potato cake. Roll in the flour and shape into small discs. Roll each
one in flaked almonds and refrigerate for at least 30 minutes;
overnight is fine.

When ready to cook, heat a good millimetre of coconut oil until hot. Fry
the potato cakes on a medium heat, until golden brown and heated
through - approximately 5 minutes on each side. When cooking a large
batch, try browning briefly then place on a large baking tray and finish
off in the oven for approximately 15-20 minutes.

———

*Tamarind is known for its high
content of the B-complex vitamin
thiamine. As well as improving
muscle development, Thiamine's
primary responsibility in humans
is to improve nerve function, which
is excellent for the brain and for
maintaining all-round ability to
stay strong and remain active.*

Indonesian gado gado

Maintain

Serves 6 as a side dish or starter

———

FOR THE SAUCE:

3 shallots, finely chopped

4 cloves of garlic, finely chopped

1cm (½") chunk of fresh galangal
(or ginger), finely chopped

2 tbsp sambal oelek (Indonesian
chilli paste) or 2 small red chillies,
deseeded and finely chopped

200g peanut butter

approx 60ml soy sauce

approx 2 tbsp coconut nectar

zest and juice of an unwaxed lime

120ml coconut milk

water

FOR THE SALAD:

1 tbsp turmeric powder

approx 200g new potatoes,
cleaned and halved

100g French green beans, trimmed

a handful each of shredded white
and green cabbage, finely sliced
red peppers and bean sprouts

a small handful of fresh coriander,
chopped

4 free-range eggs, hard-boiled

A great salad by itself and a wonderful, Asian-inspired accompaniment
to a spicy fish dish. Just close your eyes and you can hear those palm
trees rustling and feel warm sand beneath your toes!

For the sauce

In a small saucepan, gently fry the shallots, garlic, ginger and chilli until
soft. Off the heat, add all the other ingredients, except the water. Bring
this mixture up to a low simmer and stir until all the ingredients have
combined. Check the seasoning and add a little more soy
sauce and/or coconut nectar, if necessary. You are looking for the
consistency of pouring cream; so add the water, a little at a time, until
this is achieved. The sauce can be made up to a few days in advance
and stored in the fridge. It also makes a great dip for cooked chicken,
or add it to a simple stir-fry to lift the flavour.

For the salad

Add the turmeric to a large pan of water and boil the new potatoes
until just cooked, not too soft. While the potatoes are cooking, steam
(or boil) the green beans for just a few minutes. Arrange all the
vegetables onto a platter (or individual plates), top with chopped
egg and drizzle over the peanut sauce. This salad can be prepped
in advance; just add the eggs and satay at the last minute. If you are
catering for vegans, serve the egg on the side so guests can add it if
they want. The great thing about this dish is you can mix and match the
ingredients, using an array of fresh vegetables.

113

Iranian roasted vegetables with lime

Butternut squash will hit you with an abundance of vitamin A, so you'll be very glad you ate it! This root vegetable is wonderful for good eyesight, constipation issues, keeping blood pressure in check and assisting with weight loss and boosting immune system function. It is also high in vitamin C, which protects cells and speeds up healing.

Serves 6 as a side dish

3-4 tbsp coconut oil

1 tsp cumin seeds

1 tsp fennel seeds

1 tbsp coriander seeds

1 tsp ground turmeric

1 small butternut squash, deseeded and cut into thin slices (skin on)

2 red onions, cut into small chunks

2 large green or yellow bell peppers, deseeded and cut into chunks

2 courgettes, cut into thin slices

3 vine-ripened tomatoes, roughly chopped

50g raisins, soaked in hot water

juice and zest of an unwaxed lime

a handful of fresh coriander, chopped

Himalayan pink salt and pepper to season

2 limes, cut into segments to decorate

Preheat the oven to 200°C / 400°F / Gas Mark 6.

Start by frying the seeds and spices in the coconut oil; you want to release the flavours but not burn the spices as this will make them bitter to taste. Pour the hot, spiced oil into a large roasting tin and tip in the squash and onion chunks. Coat the vegetables and roast in the oven for about 10 minutes. Remove the tin and now add the remaining vegetables (except the tomatoes) and continue to roast until soft and beginning to crisp up. Drain the water off the raisins and reserve. Remove the vegetables and stir through the tomatoes, raisins, lime and coriander. Should the mixture be a little dry, add some of the reserved liquid from the raisins. Season to taste and serve with fresh lime wedges.

When cooking for a larger crowd, roast the vegetables in separate tins; that way you have more control over the cooking times and will ensure that they cook evenly.

114

Kale with red cabbage & pomegranate

Serves 6-8 as a side salad

———

½ red cabbage, finely shredded

approx 6 tbsp raw, unfiltered apple cider vinegar

6 tbsp coconut nectar

3 large handfuls kale, finely shredded

a little coconut oil

a small handful of flat leaf parsley and dill, chopped

juice of a lemon

2 cloves garlic, crushed

8 tbsp cold pressed extra virgin olive oil

3 tbsp raw, unfiltered apple cider vinegar

Himalayan pink salt and pepper

1 pomegranate, deseeded

Place the shredded red cabbage in a large bowl, cover in boiling water and add the apple cider vinegar and coconut nectar. Leave for about 10 minutes to soften. The idea is to create a slightly pickled effect - sweet, sharp and crunchy, so after the water is added, taste the liquid and add a little more vinegar and nectar, if necessary.

While the cabbage is marinating, pan-fry the kale in coconut oil for a few minutes, adding a little water to stop from burning. The kale should be slightly softened but still crunchy. Drain off any excess liquid from both the kale and the red cabbage and toss both the cabbages together with the herbs.

Make a dressing with the lemon, garlic, oil and vinegar and toss through the cabbage. Season, sprinkle over the pomegranate seeds and serve.

———

Ulcers and Alzheimer's Disease are just two of many ailments that red cabbage has been shown to treat quite effectively. Red cabbage has been found to be considerably potent in protecting cognitive activity. The amino acid glutamine, which is found in large quantities in red cabbage, is excellent for reducing pain and symptoms associated with ulcers in the gastrointestinal system.

Lentil and tomato soup with spring onion & rasam spices

Piperine is a key component of black pepper that has several amazing benefits. Alone, it can improve memory and repair cognitive malfunction, making it a very useful and simple thing to help those with dementia. However, piperine in black pepper also increases the bioavailability (the amount that can be absorbed within the body) of other spices and their constituents, such as turmeric with its prized constituent 'curcumin', which works synergistically with piperine.

Serves 4-6

FOR THE RASAM POWDER:

a little coconut oil

2 sprigs of curry leaves

2 tsp cumin seeds

3 tsp coriander seeds

3 tbsp fennel seeds

1 dried red chilli

½ tsp black peppercorns

½ tsp turmeric

FOR THE SOUP:

100g pigeon pea lentils

2 tbsp coconut oil

½ tsp cumin seeds

4 curry leaves

1cm (½") fresh ginger, crushed

2 garlic cloves, crushed

4 tomatoes, diced

6 spring onions, chopped

1 tbsp tamarind paste

1 tsp Himalayan pink salt

3 tbsp fresh coriander, chopped

For the rasam powder
Heat the coconut oil in a heavy-based frying pan on a medium heat. Fry the curry leaves until golden brown, then lift out with a slotted spoon and set aside. Next, toast all of the spices lightly and then grind it in spice mill, with the curry leaves, to a fine powder.

For the soup
Pigeon pea lentils are very common in Southern Indian cooking, but you can use split peas as a substitute. Start by boiling the lentils in plenty of water until tender. Drain and set aside. While the lentils are cooking, heat the coconut oil, add the cumin seeds and cook for a minute then add the ginger, garlic and the curry leaves. Fry for a further 2-3 minutes. Add the diced tomatoes and three quarters of the rasam powder. Turn down the heat and continue to simmer until the tomatoes begin to break down. Now add 120ml of water and the cooked pigeon pea lentils. Bring the soup to boil, cover and reduce heat to low and simmer for about 20 minutes, to infuse the flavours. Add the tamarind paste and more water, if necessary. Taste and season with salt. Cook for further 5 minutes and serve sprinkled with coriander.

Makloubeh

Nutmeg is an excellent detoxifier. It has the ability to cleanse the liver and the kidneys, where many toxins are stored. It is great for oral health and treats halitosis. For generations it has been regarded as a good tonic for sleeplessness, and more recently, studies have shown it has the capability to induce apoptosis (programmed cell death) in cancerous cells of patients with leukaemia.

Serves 6-8

---

approx 120g coconut oil, for frying

1 large aubergine and 2 courgettes, cut lengthwise into thin slices

1 red onion, sliced

1 small cauliflower, cut into small florets

2 medium carrots, thinly sliced

2 large tomatoes, sliced

250g short-grained rice, risotto is good

FOR THE LIQUID:

4 cloves garlic, crushed

1cm (½") chunk fresh ginger, grated

1 tsp each: ground coriander, cardamom, nutmeg and sweet paprika

480ml vegetable stock

2 tsp each Himalayan pink salt and pepper

This is a great centrepiece for a vegetarian meal and much less complicated than it looks! You'll need a heavy-based, deep pan (about 5L capacity) with a tight-fitting lid.

Start by frying the aubergine and courgette strips in batches, until golden brown. Repeat with the remaining vegetables (except the tomato). They should be slightly soft but not overcooked. Set the vegetables to one side and line your pan with a rough circle of baking paper. Just scrunch up a biggish circle and push into the bottom of the pan; you want it to come slightly up the sides as this will help to get the Makloubeh out intact. Now create a lattice-like case with the strips of grilled aubergine and courgette, overlapping the vegetables from the centre of the pan out and up the sides. Now layer in the cooked vegetables and tomatoes. Pour over the rice, making sure it sinks down through the cracks between the layers. Set the pan to one side and, in a separate pan, fry the garlic and ginger in a little oil. Add all the spices and the vegetable stock. Bring the liquid up to the boil and season. Now gently pour the stock over the pan of rice and vegetables until the rice is covered by a good 2-3mm of liquid (you may have some spare). Place the whole lot onto the hob and heat gently until bubbling; you don't want to boil too rigorously as this will disturb the layers. Once it begins to bubble, put on the lid and reduce to its lowest setting and continue to cook for approximately 30-35 minutes (the rice should be cooked and fluffy).

Remove the pan from the heat and allow to cool for 5 minutes or so. Take a large platter, wider than the pan lip, and lay the platter over the top of the Makloubeh. Hold the edges of the pan to the platter with tea towels and invert the platter in one go. The Makloubeh should not fall out immediately, so allow the pan to rest again for a few minutes, so gravity can do its work. Lift off the pan carefully and you should end up with a wonderful dome of griddled aubergine and courgette edged with rice. Peel off the baking paper and decorate with thin circles of red pepper and chilli.

Mohammara

Serves 4

2 large red peppers

1 tsp cumin seeds

2 cloves garlic, crushed

1 tbsp coconut oil

60g ground almonds

juice of half a lemon

1 tbsp coconut nectar

a small handful of flat leaf parsley, finely chopped

60g walnuts, roughly chopped

Set the oven to 220°C / 425°F / Gas Mark 7.

This is a wonderful dip to have with bread, to top a baked sweet potato or to serve with pan-fried fish.

Start by roasting the peppers in a hot oven until the skin is black and blistered. Remove the hot peppers and place in a bowl covered in cling film until cool; this will make it much easier to peel off the skin.

Meanwhile, toast the cumin seeds in oil and then add all the other ingredients, except the walnuts. Take the pan off the heat almost as soon as everything is mixed together and transfer into a pestle and mortar and bash it all together.

Once the peppers are cool, peel, deseed and finely chop the flesh. Mix the peppers into the main dip with the chopped walnuts. The rough texture of this dip is lovely but just blend in a food processor to get a smoother finish, if preferred. The smooth version makes a great pasta sauce.

Red bell peppers are ripe green peppers. This makes them nutritionally superior. They have a great balance of vitamins to natural sugar to fibre. They are also fairly good on the mineral content, such as manganese, potassium, zinc and magnesium. Red peppers can activate thermogenesis and increase metabolic rate, making them a simple way to help burn more calories.

time &
creativity

effort
soul

Nectarine & beetroot salad

Nectarines contain bioactive compounds which research has shown have distinct potential to combat obesity. They also possess anti-diabetic qualities that work in tandem with the anti-obesity properties that assist in metabolic repair and the decrease of oxidation, which ultimately protects the heart.

Serves 6 as a side dish

FOR THE DRESSING:

1 large beetroot

4 tbsp coconut nectar

juice of a lemon

1 tbsp wholegrain mustard

4-6 tbsp cold pressed extra virgin olive oil

a little Himalayan pink salt and pepper to taste

FOR THE SALAD:

4 nectarines or peaches

1 endive

2 large handfuls of rocket or spinach leaves

a small handful of flaked almonds or pumpkin seeds

Wash the beetroot and cut into large chunks - do not peel. Tip the beetroot into a large pan of water and boil for about 20 minutes, or until the beetroot is very soft. Drain the water from the pan and set aside to cool. Once the beetroot has cooled, blend all the dressing ingredients together. The dressing should be brightly coloured and glossy; add a little more olive oil if necessary. Season the dressing and set aside.

Meanwhile, finely slice the nectarines and carefully split the endive into leaves. Scatter the rocket and endive leaves over a large platter, followed by half the nectarines. Spoon a liberal amount of the dressing over the salad and top with the rest of the fruit. Lastly, toast the almonds or pumpkin seeds in a dry frying pan for a few minutes. Be careful not to let them burn. Scatter the nuts or seeds over the top of the finished dish and serve.

Pea & mint fritters

Like cloves, sumac ranks exceptionally high on the ORAC scale. With the ability to absorb more oxygen to protect cells, sumac is really a secret weapon of anti-aging in the spice cupboard! It is also antiemetic, antidiarrhoeal and antihaemorrhagic. It fights colds, sore throats and tuberculosis as well.

Serves 4

230g frozen peas (defrosted)

a small handful of fresh mint

2 shallots, roughly chopped

juice and zest of an unwaxed lemon

1 tsp Himalayan pink salt

1 tsp freshly ground black pepper

60g gram (chickpea) flour

1 tsp sumac

1 tsp ground cumin

coconut oil, for frying

Pulse the peas, mint, shallots and lemon in a food processor until coarsely chopped. Season to taste with salt and pepper. Sieve the gram flour over the mixture and beat in to remove any lumps. To finish, stir in the sumac and cumin, adding a little water if the batter is too thick.

Heat a large, heavy-based frying pan over a medium heat. Add a little coconut oil; you will need about a millimetre of melted oil. Spoon a large tablespoon of the pea and mint batter into the hot oil and fry on both sides until golden brown. Cook the fritters in batches, drain on kitchen paper and keep warm in the oven until they are all done.

These fritters make wonderful nibbles; make mini versions and serve with a hot tomato salsa or a yoghurt dip.

Cardamom is abundant in various minerals, vitamins and micronutrients. These include niacin, pyridoxine, riboflavin, thiamine, vitamin A, vitamin C, sodium, potassium, calcium, copper, iron, manganese, magnesium, phosphorous and zinc. It is found in several varieties, but the black seeds contained in the green pod are the most familiar. Cardamom has been shown to be good for asthma sufferers and to also improve cardiovascular health.

Persian style rice

Serves 6-8 as a side dish

———

2 tbsp coconut oil

5 cardamom pods, crushed

2 small cinnamon sticks

2 whole star anise

2 tbsp coriander seeds

1 tsp cumin seeds

1 tsp saffron threads

250g basmati rice, rinsed well

480ml water

120g wild rice

60g raw cashew nuts,
roughly chopped

A small handful each of fresh dill,
parsley and mint, chopped

A little cold pressed extra virgin
olive oil

Himalayan pink salt and pepper

Heat the oil in a large, heavy-based pan and fry off the cardamom, cinnamon, star anise, cumin and coriander seeds. Add the rice and stir through the heated oil and spices. Pour over the water, add the saffron, stir and bring the rice to the boil. Turn the hob down to its lowest heat; cover the pan with a tight fitting lid and leave. After about 5 minutes, lift the lid and give the rice a stir. Cover and cook for another 5 minutes until cooked but light and fluffy. At the same time, cook the wild rice in plenty of boiling water. This should take about 15 minutes. The grains of rice should still maintain a good bite, so check regularly and do not overcook. Once cooked, drain and rinse the wild rice in cold water and leave draining to remove any excess water.

To finish, stir the chopped cashews, herbs and 3-4 tablespoons of oil through the cooked rice. Lastly, stir through the drained wild rice, season and serve.

Potato & asparagus curry

Asparagus is excellent for pregnancy because of its high folate content. It also eases discomfort associated with PMS and can combat fatigue and even depression. In Ayurvedic therapy, asparagus is used to improve fertility because it contains hormone regulators which can assist with male and female sexual disorders. Asparagus also contains anti-tumour properties and surprisingly is a tonic for hangovers!

Serves 6

4 medium potatoes

6-8 spears of asparagus

2 tbsp coconut oil

1 tsp each of coriander, cumin and caraway seeds

1 large onion, finely chopped

2cm (1") chunk of fresh ginger, finely chopped

4 cloves garlic, chopped

3 tsp garam masala

½ tsp turmeric

½ tsp chilli flakes or powder

a pinch of cardamom powder

3 tbsp ground almonds

120ml almond milk

Himalayan pink salt and pepper to taste

a small handful of fresh coriander, chopped

Wash the potatoes and cut into small cubes - only peel if necessary or desired. Rinse them in cold water and boil in a large pan of water for about 5-8 minutes, until they begin to soften but are not cooked through. Drain and set aside. Prep the asparagus by snapping off the tough ends and chopping into large pieces.

Meanwhile, heat the coconut oil in a deep, heavy-based pan over a medium heat. Toast all the seeds for a minute or so to release their fragrance - be careful not to burn. Stir in the onion, ginger, garlic and spices and fry for a few minutes. Next, add in the prepped asparagus spears and stir-fry until they begin to soften a little. Stir through the ground almonds and the almond milk and then add in the drained potatoes. Cover and continue to simmer for 10-15 minutes, until all the vegetables are tender. Keep adding in a little water to stop the sauce from drying out too much. Season and serve, sprinkled with the coriander leaves.

Quinoa with Chinese red rice, orange & pine nuts

Serves 6-8 as a side dish

180g quinoa

200g Chinese red rice (available from Chinese supermarkets, or use wild rice)

2 large unwaxed oranges

1 medium red onion, diced

a little coconut oil, for frying

juice of a lemon

6 spring onions, thinly sliced

a small handful of toasted pine nuts

approx 60ml cold pressed extra virgin olive oil

a small handful of fresh flat leaf parsley, chopped

Himalayan pink salt and pepper to taste

Cook the rice and quinoa as per the instructions; quinoa takes approximately 10-12 minutes and the red or wild rice a little longer, 20 minutes or so. The grains should be tender but still retain a bit of a bite. Once cooked, drain off and lay out on baking sheets to cool quickly. While the rice is cooking, zest the oranges and set the zest aside in a large serving bowl. Next, segment the oranges; slice off the skin, making sure the majority of the pith is removed. Now take a sharp knife and gently slide down each of the membrane pockets to release the orange segment. This is a little laborious, but the pith and membrane are tough and bitter; the taste and texture of the dish will really benefit from this extra work. Tip the orange segments into the same bowl as the zest, reserving as much of the orange juice as possible.

Next, pan-fry the onion in a little coconut oil, until just beginning to soften. Scoop the onions into the bowl with the oranges and combine with the rice, quinoa and all the other ingredients. Season to taste and serve.

The zest of an orange is surprisingly also beneficial for human health. Owing to its natural histamine-suppressing compounds it actually makes for a useful home remedy for allergy sufferers. Additionally, orange peel actually has the ability to clear the lungs of toxins that cause respiratory problems, so don't be so quick to bin the peel next time you eat an orange!

Quinoa with wild rice, baby leeks & pomegranate

Serves 6-8 as a side dish

_____

180g quinoa

100g wild, black rice

a little coconut oil

1 small red onion, finely chopped

2 cloves garlic, crushed

zest and juice of an orange

2 baby leeks (small, thin leeks will do) thinly sliced

1 pomegranate, seeded

2-3 tbsp raw, unfiltered apple cider vinegar

approx 60ml cold pressed extra virgin olive oil

Himalayan pink salt and pepper to taste

Cook the rice and quinoa as per the instructions; quinoa takes approximately 10-12 minutes and the wild rice a little longer, 20 minutes or so. The grains should be tender but still retain a bit of a bite. Once both are cooked, drain off, rinse and lay out on baking sheets to cool quickly.

While the rice and quinoa are cooking, fry the onion and garlic in coconut oil for a few minutes. Add the orange zest and juice and the leeks while the pan is still warm but do not cook.

In a large bowl combine the rice and quinoa with all the other ingredients, season to taste and serve.

Great as a vegan main course with some griddled vegetables, this dish also makes a perfect base to mop up the sauce from a spicy tagine or curry.

_____

Leeks are members of the same family as onions and garlic. They protect against heart disease, help fight cancer and make weight loss easy as they are low in calories but have a significant amount of fibre making them quite filling. Leeks decrease risk of inflammatory diseases and contain a bioactive form of folate which is great during pregnancy.

Roasted potatoes with summer vegetables

Serves 6 as a side dish

———

a good 4-6 tbsp coconut oil

2 large sprigs of fresh rosemary

4 bay leaves

200g new potatoes, cleaned and cut in half, if necessary

2 red onions, cut into large chunks

2 large carrots, cut into diagonal slices

4 baby leeks, sliced into discs

2-4 baby turnips, washed and sliced

4-6 artichoke hearts, roughly chopped

a little cold pressed extra virgin olive oil

2 small handfuls of fresh summer herbs

Himalayan pink salt and pepper

Preheat the oven to 200°C / 400°F / Gas Mark 6.

Heat the coconut oil gently in a large roasting pan. Tip in all the vegetables and coat everything in the oil. Tuck the rosemary and bay leaves under the vegetables and roast in the oven for about 45 minutes, until soft and golden brown. Stir through the artichokes, season and serve hot, doused in a little olive oil with plenty of fresh herbs. Any leftovers can be blended to make a great soup.

Turnips might yet surprise you! These bulbous root vegetables are high in vitamin K, calcium, manganese and iron. They are filling and very palatable indeed and work very well in all kinds of dishes. They have the right type of carbohydrate but are not high in calories, so they add bulk to a salad without weighing it down.

Roasted squash with coriander & flaked almonds

A compound found in red onions, onionin A, is linked with reduction of inflammation. The anti-inflammatory effects of red onion may be beneficial for people with allergies, asthma and arthritis. Red onions contain high levels of organosulphur compounds, which may offer a protective effect against prostate, colorectal and stomach cancers.

Serves 6

approx 4 tbsp coconut oil

3 cardamom pods, crushed

1 tsp each of cumin and coriander seeds

1 tsp mustard seeds

3-4 cloves garlic, crushed

1-2 squash (butternut is good, but experiment with others too), peeled and cut into 2cm (1") chunks

2 tsp chilli flakes

2 red onions, thinly sliced

2 tsp Himalayan pink salt

approx 100g flaked almonds

2 pears, thinly sliced

a few small handfuls of fresh coriander, chopped

Set the oven to 220°C / 425°F / Gas Mark 7.

Heat the oil in a large roasting pan on a low heat. Start by frying the cardamom, cumin and coriander to release the flavours, be careful not to let them burn. After a couple of minutes add the mustard seeds and garlic, fry for a minute then toss through the squash cubes and chilli flakes. Transfer everything to a large roasting dish; ideally, the vegetables should be in a single layer to allow them to cook evenly. Slide the tin into the oven for about 30-40 minutes, or until the squash is soft but not mushy.

Meanwhile, toast the almond flakes in a dry frying pan, or under the grill - be careful; they can burn very quickly. Take the thinly sliced onion and soak in boiling water for a few minutes, drain and add 2 teaspoons of salt. Massage the salt into the onion and set aside; this takes some of the 'bite' out of the onion flavour but keeps them crunchy (if you prefer, add them to the roasting squash about halfway through the cooking time).

To assemble, season with salt and pepper, stir through the sliced pears and chopped coriander and sprinkle over the almonds.

Saffron rice with cherries & herbs

Serves 6-8 as a side dish

——

2 tbsp coconut oil

300g basmati rice, rinsed well

450ml water

5 cardamom pods, crushed

2 small cinnamon sticks

2 whole star anise

2 tsp coriander seeds

1 tsp cumin seeds

5 saffron threads infused in a very small amount of boiling water, overnight preferably

60g dried cherries or fresh cherries

a small handful each of fresh dill, parsley and mint

a little cold pressed extra virgin olive oil

Himalayan pink salt and pepper

Heat the oil in a large, heavy-based pan and fry the cardamom, cinnamon, star anise, cumin and coriander seeds. Add the rice and stir through the heated oil and spices. Pour over the water, add the saffron liquid with the threads, stir and bring the rice to the boil. Turn the hob down to its lowest heat, cover the pan with a tight-fitting lid and leave. After about 5 minutes, lift the lid and give the rice a stir. Cover and cook for another 5 minutes until cooked but light and fluffy.

Meanwhile, soak the cherries in hot water with a little lemon juice for a few minutes (or de-stone and chop, if using fresh cherries). Drain off the dried cherries, chop and mix together with the fresh herbs and oil. Stir these through the cooked rice. Season and serve.

Saffron is known to many as being the most expensive spice in the world. However, as it is very light in weight, it is relatively inexpensive to use. Saffron is known in the eastern cultures for treating mild to moderate depression. It provides menstrual relief for women who have irregular periods. Saffron is also known for helping to clear airways in asthma sufferers.

Shakshuka

Serves 4

———

3-4 tbsp coconut oil

1 tsp cumin seeds

1 tbsp coriander seeds

1-2 tsp smoked paprika

1 large red onion, finely sliced

2 large red peppers, finely sliced

2 cloves garlic, crushed

1 small chilli, finely chopped

1 jar tomato passata, or approx 350g fresh tomatoes, skinned, deseeded and chopped

juice of half a lemon

Himalayan pink salt and pepper

4 large free-range eggs

a small handful of flat leaf parsley, finely chopped

Set the oven to 200°C / 400°F / Gas Mark 6.

Heat the coconut oil in a heavy-based, deep cast iron skillet. Toast the cumin and coriander seeds in the oil until fragrant and then add the smoked paprika followed by the onions and peppers. Fry the vegetables for a few minutes until they begin to soften and then add the garlic and chilli. Once the onion mix has softened, pour in the tomatoes and lemon. Season and simmer until cooked. Now make four shallow wells in the surface of the sauce and crack in the eggs. Slide the skillet into the oven and bake until the eggs are cooked, approximately 30 minutes. Sprinkle over parsley and serve.

For a larger dish, you could try cooking off the sauce and then poaching a batch of eggs and laying them into the Shakshuka just before serving.

Spicy carrot & red onion salad with pilpelchuma

Capsaicin is the major active ingredient in cayenne pepper that gives it the signature hot kick recognisable in any chilli pepper. The list of benefits from cayenne is extremely long; it is an anti-irritant - it eases upset stomachs and ulcers, sore throats and coughs. It has been used to treat migraines, allergies, digestive issues, blood clots, joint pains and toothaches. If used topically as a poultice, it can treat snake bites, sores and wounds.

Serves 6 as a side dish

FOR THE PILPELCHUMA (SPICE PASTE):

2 whole heads of garlic

1 dried Ancho chilli (this adds a lovely smoky note to the paste but ordinary chilli will do)

1 tbsp each of cayenne pepper and sweet paprika (try using smoked if you can't get hold of Ancho chillies)

1 tbsp each of cumin and caraway seeds, roughly ground in a pestle and mortar

juice of a lemon or lime

FOR THE SALAD:

6 large carrots, peeled and cut into thin diagonal slices (a mandolin is best the get the right diameter)

2 tbsp coconut oil

1 sweet potato, washed and cut into thin batons

2-3 red onions, thinly sliced

zest of an unwaxed orange and a little juice

approx 200g of salad leaves: rocket, spinach, watercress etc

Start by making the Pilpelchuma paste. Break the garlic heads into cloves and wrap in tin foil (no need to peel). Roast in a hot oven for at least 30 minutes, or until soft and caramelised.

In the meantime, soak the Ancho chilli in a little hot water.

Allow the roasted garlic to cool a little then squeeze the softened bulbs into a food processor.

Roughly chop the soaked chilli, reserving the water, and add this, with all the other ingredients, to the garlic.

Blend until smooth, using the reserved chilli water to moisten the paste if necessary. Any leftover after using in the salad can be kept in a jar in the fridge.

Cook the carrots in plenty of water; they need to be al dente, and the cooking time will depend on the thickness of the slices, so watch carefully. Once cooked, drain and refresh in cold water to stop the cooking process.

Once the carrots are cooked, heat the coconut oil in a heavy-based frying pan and fry the sweet potato until golden brown. Next, add the onion, with approximately 1 tbsp of the chilli paste. Continue to fry until caramelised and soft. Stir in the orange zest followed by the carrots. Taste and season. It may need a little orange or lemon juice to adjust the acidity. Gently toss the carrot mixture through the salad leaves and serve.

Spicy tomato soup tempered with garlic, roasted cumin & basil

Serves 4

———

3 tbsp coconut oil

2 tsp cumin seed

3 garlic cloves, crushed

1cm (½") fresh ginger, finely chopped

1 mild green chilli, deseeded and chopped

8-10 ripened tomatoes, diced

½ tsp turmeric powder

Himalayan pink salt and pepper to taste

a small handful of fresh basil, chopped

Heat the coconut oil in a deep, heavy-based pan over a medium heat. Dry-fry the cumin seeds for a few minutes and then tip into a mortar and roughly grind. Return half the crushed seeds to the pan and add the garlic, ginger and chopped chilli. Sauté the mixture for 1-2 minutes and then add the diced tomato and turmeric. Bring the pan up to a gentle boil and cook until the tomatoes start to break up. Stir in enough water to cover the tomatoes, cover and simmer for about 20 minutes. Once the soup is finished, use a hand blender to blend the soup. Taste and adjust the seasoning and serve with chopped basil and a sprinkle of the remaining toasted cumin seeds.

You can pass the tomato mixture through a sieve if you prefer; this will remove any traces of tomato skin for a silkier finish to the soup.

———

The famed compound within turmeric that has some powerful health benefits is the one known as 'curcumin'. Curcumin is heralded as a 'natural wonder drug' since it has the ability and potential to relieve symptoms of pain, inflammation and even some diseases. In multiple studies curcumin has been shown to reduce the growth of cancerous cells and prevent tumours from growing new blood vessels to feed themselves and has even been seen to cause cancer cell death. Turmeric is better absorbed into the blood stream when combined with black pepper as their respective compounds enhance each other's efficacy.

Stuffed roasted peppers

Rosemary boosts the immune system, improves mood and stress and increases intelligence and focus through improved memory. Research has found that effects on brain function are improved with regular consumption of rosemary leaves as opposed to simply a few leaves every so often. Rosemary is also a stomach soother and a breath freshener.

Serves 6 as a main dish

approx 4 tbsp coconut oil

1 large onion, finely chopped

3 garlic cloves, crushed

2 bay leaves

2-4 sprigs fresh rosemary

1 medium swede, peeled and cut into 1cm (½") dice

4 medium carrots, peeled and cut into 1cm (½") dice

4 tbsp capers, drained and roughly chopped

6 large red, yellow or orange peppers

Himalayan pink salt and pepper

approx 4cm (2") cube of feta cheese (optional)

a small handful of fresh flat leaf parsley, roughly chopped

Set oven to 220°C / 425°F / Gas Mark 7.

Start by heating the coconut oil in a deep, heavy-based pan and frying the onion, garlic and herbs for a few minutes. Next, toss through the diced vegetables, turn down the heat and continue to sauté, until soft and caramelised. Occasionally add a little water or vegetable stock to stop everything from sticking to the pan. Once the vegetables are cooked, stir through the capers.

Meanwhile, halve the peppers lengthwise and lay on a large baking sheet lined with baking paper. Roast in the oven for approximately 30 minutes or until slightly charred and soft. Remove from the oven and set aside.

Remove the woody herbs from the swede and carrot mix and roughly mash everything together. Taste and season with salt and pepper. Load the peppers with this stuffing and crumble over the feta cheese. Pop back in the oven until the cheese begins to colour (a hot grill works well too). Remove and serve sprinkled with parsley.

Sweet potato with cardamom & nigella seeds

Serves 6

---

approx 4 tbsp coconut oil

1 large cinnamon stick

2 whole star anise

3 cardamom pods, crushed

1 fresh chilli, finely chopped

3 cloves garlic, crushed

2-3 red onions, thinly sliced

1 tsp each of ground cumin and coriander

approx 5-6 medium-sized sweet potatoes, washed and cut into 2cm (1") chunks

2 tsp nigella seeds

approx 60-90ml vegetable stock

a handful of fresh coriander, chopped

Set the oven to 220°C / 425°F / Gas Mark 7.

Heat the oil in a heavy-based pan on a medium heat. Start by frying the cinnamon, star anise and cardamom to release the flavours - be careful not to let them burn. After a couple of minutes, add the chilli, garlic, onions, cumin and coriander. Allow the onions and spices to cook for a few more minutes and then toss through the sweet potato and nigella seeds. Transfer everything to a deep roasting tin; ideally, the vegetables should be in a single layer to allow them to cook evenly. Pour half the stock over the sweet potato mix and slide into the oven for about 30 minutes, or until the potato is soft but not mushy and starting to brown. Check halfway through the cooking time and add a little more stock if necessary. Once the sweet potatoes are cooked, rest the tin for 5-10 minutes to allow the remaining liquid to be absorbed. Scatter over the chopped coriander and serve.

If you only need a small batch, this can be done completely in the frying pan; just keep a little water or stock handy, sloshing in a little every few minutes to keep the contents from burning and sticking to the pan.

The number of ailments that mustard seeds improve the symptoms of are well over 20 common ones. Mustard seeds can help with skin infections, colds, muscle and back pain, menopausal symptoms, high blood pressure, migraines, rheumatoid arthritis, atherosclerosis, respiratory congestion and poor digestion... and that's just the beginning of the list!

"The food you eat can be either the safest and most powerful
form of medicine or the slowest form of poison."
Ann Wigmore

Sweet potato with olives & chickpeas

Olives contain some very important nutrients, the most notable one being oleic acid, which is a monounsaturated fatty acid which is cited as reducing blood pressure and the risk of cardiovascular disease. Olives also contain high amounts of selenium, zinc and vitamin E, which protect cells.

Serves 6 as a side dish

4 medium-sized sweet potatoes

1-2 tsp smoked paprika

coconut oil

1 carton chickpeas, drained and rinsed

approx 100g pitted green olives

1 small red onion, finely chopped

1-2 red chillies, deseeded and finely sliced

a drizzle of cold pressed extra virgin olive oil

Himalayan pink salt and pepper to taste

Set the oven to 220°C / 425°F / Gas Mark 7.

Start by washing the sweet potatoes (leave the skin on) and cutting into fat wedges. Take a large roasting tin, sit it over a low heat and melt approximately 3 tablespoons of coconut oil with the smoked paprika. Toss the sweet potatoes into the spiced oil and roast in the oven for approximately half an hour, or until the potatoes are golden brown and soft. Remove the roasting tin from the oven and stir in the drained chickpeas. Meanwhile, mix the olives with some olive oil, the red onion and the sliced chillies. When ready to serve, pour this mixture over the potatoes, check the seasoning and transfer to a large serving dish.

Tomato and red onion in sweet tamarind masala

Fenugreek seeds have been reported to assist with the control of type II diabetes owing to the presence of the natural fibre galactomannan. Fenugreek slows down the rate at which sugar is absorbed into the bloodstream. A particular amino acid (4-hydroxyisoleucine) in fenugreek induces the production of insulin, so just 15-20 grams of fenugreek a day can impact blood sugar levels positively.

Serves 6

2-3 tbsp coconut oil

½ tsp fenugreek seeds

1 tsp nigella seeds

2 tsp ground coriander

1 large onion, finely chopped

2cm (1") chunk fresh ginger, grated

4 cloves garlic, crushed

1-2 chillies, deseeded and finely chopped

2 red onions, thinly sliced

8-10 large vine-ripened tomatoes, roughly chopped

6 tbsp desiccated coconut

4 tbsp raisins

2 tbsp coconut nectar

3 tsp tamarind paste

Himalayan pink salt and pepper to taste

a small handful of fresh coriander, chopped

This is a wonderful blend of hot, sweet and sour flavours which makes the dish very moreish. A firm favourite at Eliane - a comforting main for vegans, which is often nabbed by the meat eaters as well!

Heat the coconut oil in a heavy-based, deep frying pan over a medium heat. Tip in the seeds and fry for a few minutes to release their aroma - be careful not to burn. Next add in the ground coriander, onion, ginger and chilli, turn down the heat a little and fry until the onion is soft, adding a little water from time to time to stop everything from sticking. Once the sauce is well combined, add the red onion and continue to fry until the onion is just beginning to soften. Next, tip in the tomatoes, desiccated coconut, raisins, coconut nectar and tamarind paste. Stir well, cover and simmer on a low heat for 10 minutes. Taste and adjust the seasoning with salt, pepper, coconut nectar and tamarind paste until it is to your liking. The sauce should be thick, a coating rather than a soup; if the sauce is too thin, uncover the pan and turn up the heat to cook off some of the liquid. Scatter over the fresh coriander and serve.

Vegetable biryani

Maintain

Serves 6-8

___

FOR THE CURRY:

approx 60g coconut oil

2 bay leaves

2 medium onions, finely sliced

1 tsp cumin seeds

4 green cardamom pods, crushed

4 whole cloves

2cm (1") cinnamon stick

6 garlic cloves, crushed

1cm (½") chunk of fresh ginger, grated

1 tsp each of ground cumin and ground coriander

¼ tsp chilli flakes

½ tsp turmeric

2 large potatoes cut into 2cm (1") chunks

1 sweet potato cut into 2cm (1") chunks

100g frozen peas

2 tbsp tomato purée

1 tbsp fresh lemon juice

a small handful of fresh coriander, chopped

2 bell peppers (1 green and 1 red), thinly sliced

a small handful of fresh mint, chopped

Himalayan pink salt to taste

FOR THE RICE:

2cm (1") cinnamon stick

1 tsp fennel seeds

1 tsp cumin seeds

1 whole star anise

1 bay leaf

4 whole cloves

300g basmati rice

2 tsp Himalayan pink salt

Preheat oven to 180°C/ 350°F / Gas Mark 4.

Start by checking the ingredients list and prepping all the vegetables, fruit and nuts.

In a heavy-based pan heat the oil over a medium heat and add the bay leaves and onions. Fry for a few minutes, and, as the onion starts to turn golden, add the whole spices. Continue to fry for 2-3 minutes and add the ground spices, followed by the garlic and ginger. Continue to cook for further 4 minutes, adding a little water if the mixture starts to stick. Add in the potatoes, peas, tomato purée, lemon juice and half the coriander. Pour in approximately 60ml of water, cover and simmer for about 20 minutes, until potatoes are almost cooked. The mixture should resemble a fairly dry curry so just add a little water as it cooks to stop the curry burning onto the bottom of the pan. After about 20 minutes, add the peppers, mint and the rest of the coriander. Continue to simmer for another 5 minutes, season and leave the dish to rest while you prepare the rice.

Begin to heat a large pan of water (approximately 2 litres). Add all the spices and bring to the boil. Add the rice and salt and simmer until the grain is three quarters cooked (the rice should still be slightly hard). Strain the rice through a colander and leave for a few minutes to ensure all the water has drained off.

To assemble the biryani, spread about a third of the rice over the base of a large casserole dish and spoon a third of the curry over the rice. Repeat the layers, scattering some of the almonds, apricots and a sprinkle of rosewater between each layer. Cover the casserole with a lid and bake in the oven for 20 minutes, or until the rice is soft.

TO FINISH:

12 dried apricots soaked in warm water, drained and chopped

20 whole almonds soaked in water for 45 minutes, drained and skinned

3 tbsp rose water (optional)

160

Garlic is a vegetable that has been used for centuries, not only for its taste but for its wealth of medicinal uses and benefits. Garlic is antibacterial, antifungal, antiviral, anti-inflammatory and antiparasitic. In fact, it has a range of supporting nutrients that enable it to support immune system health in a way not matched by other vegetables, and bacteria cannot build up a resistance to garlic's unique make-up.

Watercress & herb salad with eggs Maintain

Serves 6-8

_____

6 free-range eggs, boiled, peeled and quatered

FOR THE DRESSING:

2 garlic cloves, crushed

2-4 tbsp fresh lemon juice

6-8 tbsp cold pressed extra virgin olive oil

Himalayan pink salt and pepper

FOR THE SALAD:

a small handful each of fresh herbs: dill, basil, mint and coriander

6-8 large handfuls of watercress

50g fresh coconut, thinly sliced

2 handfuls of fresh rocket leaves

TO FINISH:

2 tbsp flaked almonds

2 tbsp pumpkin seeds

2 tsp sesame seeds

½ tsp cumin seeds

1 tsp nigella seeds

½ tsp chilli flakes

¼ tsp Himalayan pink salt

To make the dressing, whisk together the garlic, lemon juice, olive oil and a little salt and pepper. Taste and adjust the seasoning if necessary.

Assemble the salad by gently mixing watercress and herbs together with most of the dressing. Reserve any that is left over.

Toast all of the seeds, together with the salt, in a dry pan for approximately 2-3 minutes. Keep a close eye on the nuts and seeds so they do not burn! Allow the seeds to cool and then scatter over the watercress salad, add the eggs and serve.

The salad works really well without the eggs for a vegan version, or simply serve the eggs on the side, if feeding a crowd.

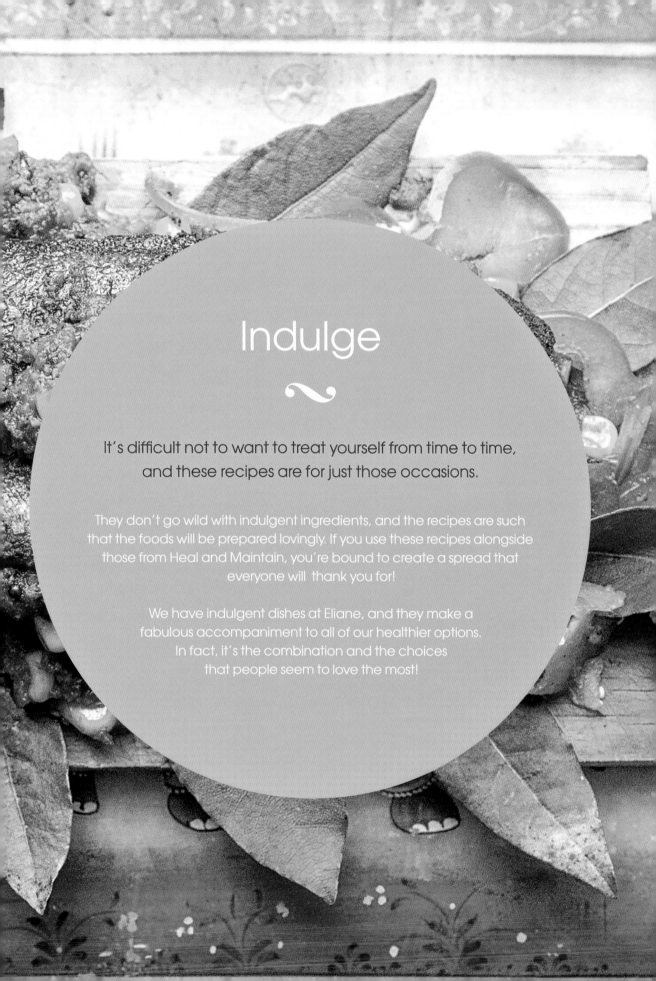

Indulge

~

It's difficult not to want to treat yourself from time to time,
and these recipes are for just those occasions.

They don't go wild with indulgent ingredients, and the recipes are such
that the foods will be prepared lovingly. If you use these recipes alongside
those from Heal and Maintain, you're bound to create a spread that
everyone will thank you for!

We have indulgent dishes at Eliane, and they make a
fabulous accompaniment to all of our healthier options.
In fact, it's the combination and the choices
that people seem to love the most!

Bombay fish curry

Serves 4-6

———

3-4 tbsp coconut oil

1 tsp each of coriander, black mustard, fenugreek and cumin seeds

½ tsp turmeric powder

1 tsp garam masala

2 chillies, finely chopped

3-4 cloves garlic, crushed

4cm (2") chunk fresh ginger, grated

1 large onion, finely chopped

2 tbsp tamarind paste (or the juice of a lime)

approx 350g tomatoes, chopped (or a jar of passata, approx 350g)

30-40g desiccated coconut

4-6 salmon fillets, or any other firm fish, cut into large chunks

Himalayan pink salt and pepper to taste

a handful of fresh coriander, chopped

Tamarind can be bought in most speciality supermarkets and usually comes in a block. To reconstitute it, cover in boiling water and allow the tamarind to soften. Take care; even if the tamarind is labelled stone free, you may need to remove a few large stones (a bit like a plum stone). Once soft, mash with a fork or blitz in a food processor. Tamarind adds a unique sharp, salty and fruity flavour.

Heat the oil in a heavy-based, deep pan over a medium heat. First add the whole spices and fry for a few minutes to release the flavours (do not burn, as they will become very bitter). Now add the powdered spices followed by the chilli, garlic, ginger and onion. Continue to cook until the onion softens; add a little water if it begins to stick to the pan. Now add the tamarind, tomatoes and desiccated coconut. Cook for 5-10 minutes until the coconut has thickened the sauce. It may be necessary to add a little water; it depends on how much juice the tomatoes release. Add the fish pieces and stir gently until the fish is coated in the sauce. Turn up the heat and continue to simmer for 2-4 minutes or until the fish is cooked through. Serve hot, scattered with coriander.

Broccoli gratin

Serves 6 as a side dish

_____

2 heads of fresh broccoli, separated into florets

100g mozzarella cheese, grated

100g mature cheddar cheese, grated

1 tbsp grated fresh ginger

½ mild green chilli, deseeded and finely chopped

3 tbsp fresh coriander stalk, chopped

½ tsp ground cardamom

8 tbsp thick Greek yogurt

½ tsp each Himalayan pink salt and pepper

2 tbsp coconut oil

Boil a large pan of water and blanch the broccoli florets for one minute. There is no need to completely cook the broccoli as it will continue cooking in the oven later. Drain the pan and plunge the florets in cold water to stop the cooking process. Next, mix together all of the other ingredients in a large bowl. Drain off the broccoli, shaking off all the excess water, and tip into the bowl with the cheese, yoghurt, herbs and spices. Coat the florets well and marinate for about an hour.

Take a large, ovenproof gratin dish and rub the coconut oil over its surface. Tip the broccoli and the marinade into the dish and roast for approximately 15-20 minutes, or until the surface is golden brown.

Chicken & apricot curry

Serves 6

_____

3-4 tbsp coconut oil

1 tsp each of coriander and cumin seeds

2 cardamom pods, bruised with a rolling pin

1 cinnamon stick

½ tsp turmeric powder

1 tsp garam masala

½ tsp ground cloves

2 chillies, finely chopped

3-4 cloves garlic, crushed

4cm (2″) chunk fresh ginger, grated

1 large onion, finely chopped

approx 350g tomatoes, chopped (or a jar of passata)

4-6 large chicken breasts or 8-12 chicken thighs, trimmed and cut into chunks

150g soft, dried apricots

2 tbsp raw, unfiltered apple cider vinegar

a handful of fresh coriander, chopped

Heat the oil in a heavy-based, deep pan over a medium heat. First add the whole spices and fry for a few minutes to release the flavours (do not burn, as they will become very bitter). Now add the powdered spices followed by the chilli, garlic, ginger and onion. Continue to cook until the onion softens. Now add the tomatoes and cook for 5 minutes.

Add the chicken pieces, apricots and apple cider vinegar; stir well until the chicken is coated in the sauce, turn up the heat and continue to simmer for 15 minutes, or until the chicken is cooked through. Should the sauce become a little dry, add some water or simply put a lid on the pot. When ready to eat, remove the cinnamon stick and cardamom pods. Serve hot, scattered with coriander.

Try cooking the spices and onion and keep them in the fridge. That way you have a ready-made paste to whip up a quick curry whenever it's needed. A great way to use up leftover fish, chicken or vegetables.

Chicken kofta with beetroot & yoghurt dressing

Serves 6-8 as a main dish

_____

FOR THE DRESSING:

2 beetroot bulbs (approx 400g), washed and cut into large chunks

1 tsp cumin seeds

8 tbsp thick Greek yoghurt

1 tbsp raw, unfiltered apple cider vinegar

Himalayan pink salt and pepper

FOR THE KOFTAS:

1 large onion, finely chopped

approx 800g minced chicken

small handful each of fresh flat leaf parsley and coriander, chopped

1cm (½") chunk of fresh ginger, finely chopped

2 large cloves of garlic, crushed

juice of a small lime

1 tsp each of ground cumin, cinnamon and nutmeg

2 chillies, deseeded and finely chopped

1 free-range egg, beaten

2 tbsp gram flour or rice flour

1 tsp each of Himalayan pink salt and ground black pepper

coconut oil, for frying

Preheat the oven to 200°C / 400°F / Gas Mark 6.

Start by making the dressing. Boil the beetroot in plenty of water until soft. Drain the beetroot and allow them to cool. Once they are cool enough to handle, slide off the skin, tip the beetroot into a food processor and purée until smooth. In a small frying pan over a medium heat, toast the cumin seeds for a few minutes. Once the cumin seeds release their aroma, remove the pan from the heat and stir in the rest of the ingredients. Check the seasoning and reserve the dressing for later.

Next, fry the onion in a little coconut oil until soft. Tip the fried onion, along with all the remaining ingredients, into a large bowl. Knead the mixture to make sure the onion, herbs, spices, lime juice, egg, flour and seasoning are evenly distributed. The mixture should hold together easily, so add a little more flour if necessary.

Heat a few tablespoons of coconut oil in a heavy-based frying pan until a small dollop of the kofta mix bubbles when added to the pan. Shape the kofta into small patties (about 4cm (2") in diameter) and fry on each side until golden brown. Cook off the patties in batches, if necessary, and set onto a large baking tray lined with foil or baking paper. Once all the kofta are browned, cover the baking tray with tin foil (this will keep them moist). Slide the tray into the oven and cook for a further 15-20 minutes (or until cooked through; the thinner the kofta the quicker they will cook).

Serve the beetroot and yoghurt dressing in a bowl, surrounded by the kofta. You can make the kofta mix and the dressing a few days in advance. They also make great bite-sized canapés.

Chicken meatballs with tomato & harissa

Serves 6-8 as a main dish

⎯⎯⎯

FOR THE MEATBALLS:

approx 700-800g minced chicken

1 large onion, finely chopped

small handful each of fresh flat leaf
parsley and coriander, chopped

2 large cloves of garlic, crushed

1 tsp ground cumin

2 chillies, deseeded and
finely chopped

1 free-range egg, beaten

2 tbsp gram flour or rice flour

1 tsp each Himalayan pink salt
and ground black pepper

coconut oil, for frying

FOR THE SAUCE:

1 tsp coriander seeds

a little coconut oil

1 red onion, chopped

3 cloves garlic, finely chopped

2 preserved lemons, finely chopped

2 tbsp harissa paste (see page 108)

2 tbsp fresh oregano, chopped

1 large jar of tomato passata

Himalayan pink salt and pepper

Preheat the oven to 200°C / 400°F / Gas Mark 6.
(The oven is only necessary if you want to finish cooking the completed dish in the oven.)

To make the meatballs, simply put all the ingredients into a large bowl and knead until completely combined. Roll into small balls, about 2-3cm (1") in diameter, and set aside on a baking sheet. Heat about 5mm (1/4") of coconut oil in a wide frying pan and lightly brown off the meatballs on each side. Drain on sheets of kitchen paper and set aside until needed.

Heat a heavy-based, deep frying pan on a medium heat and dry-fry the coriander seeds for a few minutes, being careful not to let them burn. Add a little coconut oil to the pan and add the onions and garlic. Fry gently for a few minutes until soft then add the preserved lemons and harissa. Coat the onion mixture in the paste then add the tomatoes and herbs. Stir well and season to taste. Simmer for about 5 minutes and then add the meatballs. Cover and continue to simmer for another 8-10 minutes, or until the meatballs are cooked through. If you prefer (and your pan can go in the oven) then you can finish this dish off there.

Chicken with dates & olives

Serves 6-8 as a main dish

——

6-8 large chicken breasts or 12-16 thighs, skinned and boned

2 large onions, chopped

1cm (½") chunk of fresh ginger, finely chopped

3 large cloves of garlic, crushed

zest and juice of an unwaxed lemon

1 tsp each of ground cumin, cinnamon and nutmeg

1 tsp chilli flakes

2 tbsp gram (chickpea) flour

100g pitted dates, chopped

100g pitted green and black olives, chopped

Himalayan pink salt and pepper to taste

Preheat the oven to 200°C / 400°F / Gas Mark 6.

Start by chopping the chicken into bite-sized chunks, removing any excess fat and skin. Heat a deep, heavy-based pan on a medium heat and fry the chicken with the onions, followed by the ginger, garlic, lemon and spices and continue to fry until the chicken begins to colour. Add the flour and cook for a few minutes to form a sauce with the pan juices; add a little water if necessary. Finally, stir in the dates and olives, cover the pan and cook for a further 10 minutes until the chicken is cooked through and the flavours have infused. Adjust the seasoning and serve with rice.

Courgette & cheese bake

Serves 4-6

———

2-4 tbsp coconut oil

1 medium red onion, thinly sliced

2 cloves garlic, crushed

½ tsp cumin seeds

4 medium-sized courgettes, sliced

2 sprigs of oregano, chopped finely

4 large tomatoes, thinly sliced

150g grated cheddar cheese

a small handful of fresh flat leaf parsley, chopped

a small handful of fresh basil, chopped

a pinch of Himalayan pink salt and freshly ground black pepper

Set the oven to 200°C / 400°F / Gas Mark 6.

Heat a little coconut oil in a large, heavy-based frying pan over a medium heat. Sauté the onion and garlic until lightly brown. Add the cumin seeds and the courgette slices and continue to fry until the courgettes begin to soften. Stir through the fresh oregano and season to taste.

In an ovenproof dish, layer the courgette mixture alternately with the sliced tomatoes and half the grated cheese. Top the dish with the remaining cheese and half the herbs and bake for 20 minutes, or until golden brown. Serve hot with the rest of the herbs scattered on top.

Curried South Indian eggs

Serves 6 as a side dish

———

6 free-range eggs, hard-boiled, peeled and halved

2 tbsp coconut oil

1 tsp mustard seeds

1 medium onion, finely chopped

1 small cinnamon stick

1 mild green chilli, deseeded and finely chopped

3-4 tomatoes, roughly chopped

1cm (½") chunk of ginger, finely chopped

½ tsp turmeric powder

¼ tsp mild chilli powder

1 tsp coriander powder

1 tsp tamarind paste

120ml coconut milk

8-10 curry leaves

Himalayan pink salt to taste

a small handful of fresh coriander, chopped

To make the sauce, heat the oil in a heavy-based saucepan over a medium heat. Add the mustard seeds to the hot oil and let them splutter for a few seconds before tipping in the onions and fry for 2-3 minutes. Next, add the cinnamon stick and green chillies, frying for a further minute. Pour in the chopped tomatoes and cook for 3-4 minutes, stirring well to ensure the mixture does not stick to the bottom of the pan. The tomatoes will soften and form a thick paste. Add the ginger and fry for a further minute, then add the powdered spices and stir for a few minutes. At this point the oil will start to leave the sides of the pan. Add the tamarind paste along with a splash of water.

At this point, the spicy paste can be reserved to use in any dish: soups, curries, stir-fries etc. A favourite lunch dish is spicy scrambled eggs: simply fry a tablespoon of the paste in a little coconut oil, pour in 2-3 eggs and stir until cooked.

To finish the sauce, bring the spicy tomato paste up to the boil, then add the coconut milk and curry leaves. Reduce the heat and continue to simmer to infuse the flavours. After 5 minutes, tip in the halved, boiled eggs and let the eggs soak in the spices. Stir gently, making sure the eggs stay intact and continue to cook for 5 minutes or so, until the eggs have warmed through. Season to taste and serve garnished with coriander.

Fish cakes with apple & mint raita

Indulge

Serves 4 as a main dish

FOR THE RAITA:

1 tsp cumin seeds

200g thick Greek yoghurt

large apple, grated

a small handful of fresh mint,
chopped

1 tbsp raw, unfiltered apple
cider vinegar

Himalayan pink salt and pepper
to taste

FOR THE FISH CAKES:

approx 800g fish (e.g. salmon,
monkfish, cod etc)

small handful each of fresh mint,
parsley and dill, chopped

1cm (½") chunk of fresh ginger,
finely chopped

2 large cloves of garlic, crushed

zest of a small unwaxed lime
(keep the juice to squeeze over
the fish cakes)

1 tsp each of ground cumin,
coriander and turmeric

1 free-range egg, beaten

2 tbsp gram flour or rice flour

1 tsp each of Himalayan pink salt
and ground black pepper

coconut oil, for frying

Preheat the oven to 200°C / 400°F / Gas Mark 6.

Make the raita by dry frying the cumin seeds until fragrant and mix into
all the other ingredients. Season to taste and set aside until needed.

Cut the fish into a small dice (firm white fish is good but remember that
this is a great recipe to use up odds and ends of fish and shellfish from
other dishes). Add all the remaining ingredients and mix well; the
mixture should hold together easily, so add a little more flour, if
necessary. Ideally, rest the mixture for at least an hour to allow the
flour to bind with the other ingredients; the fish cakes will hold
together much better.

Heat a few tablespoons of coconut oil in a heavy-based frying pan
over a medium heat, until a small dollop of the fish cake mix bubbles
when added to the oil. Shape the fish mixture into small patties (about
4cm in diameter) and fry on each side until golden brown. Cook the
cakes in batches, if necessary, and set onto a large baking tray lined
with foil or baking paper. Place the baking sheet into the oven and
cook for a further 8 minutes (or until cooked through; the thinner the
cakes the quicker they will cook).

Serve the apple raita in a bowl surrounded by the fish cakes. You can
make the fish cake mix and the raita a few days in advance, although
only add the grated apple to the raita at the last minute, otherwise it
will discolour. The fish cakes also make great bite-sized canapés.

182

Herb crusted griddled prawns

Serves 4 as a main dish

12 large, shell on prawns

FOR THE MARINADE:

4cm (2") chunk of ginger, finely chopped

10 garlic cloves, crushed

2 sticks of lemongrass, finely chopped

1 mild green chilli, deseeded and finely chopped

a small handful of fresh mint, chopped

a small handful of raw cashew nuts

juice and zest of 1 unwaxed lemon

½ tsp of Himalayan pink salt

½ tsp of cumin powder

a pinch of black pepper

Set the oven 200°C/ 400°F / Gas Mark 6.

Tip all of the marinade ingredients into a large pestle and mortar and bash until a rough paste is formed. Alternatively, blend together all the ingredients in a food processor.

Smother the marinade all over the prawns generously. Cover and refrigerate for at least an hour to allow the marinade to infuse.

When ready to cook, heat a large griddle pan over a high heat and griddle the prawns, 4 at a time, on a very hot griddle for 3-4 minutes. Lift the griddled prawns onto a baking sheet lined with baking paper and continue to cook, in the oven, for approximately 8 minutes, to make sure they are cooked through.

Lavender & honey glazed chicken

Indulge

Serves 4

FOR THE GLAZE:

5 tbsp fresh orange juice

1 tsp raw, unfiltered apple
cider vinegar

3 tbsp runny honey
or coconut nectar

1 tsp dried lavender

1 bay leaf

2 sprigs of rosemary, about 2cm
long, finely chopped

4 chicken breasts, on the bone

TO FINISH:

6 tbsp pine nuts, lightly toasted

a handful of chopped chives

Heat the oven to 190°C / 375°F / Gas Mark 5.

About an hour in advance, heat all the ingredients for the glaze
together in a small pan. Simmer the glaze for a few minutes, then
allow to rest and the herbs to infuse.

Start the chicken by setting the roasting tin over a medium heat on the
hob and add the chicken, skin side down, and fry until golden brown.
Off the heat, turn the breasts over and paint on the glaze. Cover in tin
foil and cook in the oven for approximately 30-40 minutes, or until, when
skewered, the chicken juices run clear, not pink. Allow the meat to rest
for 5 minutes then scatter over the pine nuts and chives and serve with
the pan juices.

grow it with love

~

prepare it with care

~

enjoy it with passion

~

share it with joy

Lawar kachang

Serves 6 as a main dish

———

FOR THE SPICE PASTE:

120g raw cashew nuts

1 tsp black pepper

2 tsp shrimp paste (optional)

1-2 red chillies, deseeded and sliced

2 tbsp turmeric powder

2 sticks of lemongrass, finely chopped

2cm (1") chunk galangal (Thai ginger) or fresh ginger, finely chopped

FOR THE MAIN DISH:

approx 6-8 tbsp coconut oil

500g minced chicken

2 tbsp palm sugar or honey

approx 300g French green beans

5 shallots, finely sliced

2 red onions, finely diced

6 cloves of garlic, finely chopped

1-2 birdseye chillies, deseeded and chopped (leave out if you prefer less spicy heat)

approx 100g grated fresh coconut (or 60g desiccated coconut if you can't get fresh)

juice of 2 limes

2 tbsp fish sauce

In a pestle and mortar, pound all the spice paste ingredients together until they form a rough paste. The paste can be made in advance and either frozen or kept in the fridge for up to a week. A quick alternative is to roughly chop the lemongrass and galangal (or ginger) and blend in a food processor.

In a large bowl, mix together the spice paste, chicken mince and palm sugar until well combined.

Heat 2-3 tbsp of the coconut oil in the wok and stir-fry the chicken mixture until cooked through. Set the chicken aside to cool; if necessary, refrigerate until needed.

While the chicken is cooking, set a large pan of salted water on to boil. Wash and trim the green beans and blanch in boiling water for a few minutes - be careful not to overcook. Drain and rinse the beans under cold water to halt the cooking process. Cut the beans into pieces approximately 2cm (1") in length, and set them aside.

When ready to eat, heat 2 tbsp coconut oil in a wok over a high heat and fry the shallots until crispy, then transfer to absorbent paper to soak up the excess oil. Reheat the wok with a little more oil, if necessary, and stir-fry the onions, garlic and chilli until soft. Now add in the cooked chicken and green beans and fry until heated through. Tip the hot chicken into a serving dish and scatter over the grated coconut and fried shallots. Lastly, create a dressing with the lime juice and fish sauce, pour over the dish and serve.

Moroccan chicken salad

Serves 4

———

2 tbsp coconut oil

4 chicken breasts (or 6-8 chicken thighs), skinned, boned and cut into bite-sized chunks

1 red onion, finely sliced

2 cloves garlic, crushed

1cm (½") fresh ginger, finely chopped

1 tsp coriander seeds

1 tsp each of ground cinnamon and nutmeg

1-2 tbsp harissa paste (see page 108) - add more or less, depending on how spicy you like it

about 100g thick, natural Greek yoghurt

1 large mango, peeled and chopped

½ cucumber, diced

Himalayan pink salt and pepper to taste

a handful per person of baby leaf; lamb's lettuce, spinach, watercress etc

This is a take on a traditional coronation chicken, replacing the Indian spices and mayonnaise with a Moroccan influence and a healthier yoghurt dressing. To make it dairy free, just replace the yoghurt with a dash of cold pressed extra virgin olive oil and a little organic apple cider vinegar. This is a perfect dish for a large gathering; make it in advance and refrigerate until needed.

Heat the oil in a heavy-based frying pan on a medium heat and pan fry the chicken pieces until cooked through, then remove and reserve in a large bowl. Next fry the onion, adding the garlic, ginger, coriander seeds and ground spices after a couple of minutes; the onions should be slightly soft but still retain some bite and a good colour. Scoop the onion mixture into a separate bowl, adding the harissa paste, yoghurt, mango and cucumber. Adjust the seasoning and add the chicken pieces, making sure any excess juices are strained off.

Serve the salad, either warm or cold, on a bed of leaves.

Nut & herb crusted tuna with a peach & red onion salsa

Serves 4-6

———

FOR THE SALSA:

2 large ripe peaches, diced

1 large ripe mango, peeled and diced

1 medium red onion, finely chopped

1 mild red chilli, seeded and finely chopped

a small handful of fresh coriander, chopped

4 tbsp cold pressed extra virgin olive oil

1 tbsp of pure honey or coconut nectar

juice and zest of 2 unwaxed limes

Himalayan pink salt and black pepper to taste

FOR THE NUT CRUST:

a small handful each of fresh, flat leaf parsley and coriander

2 tbsp fresh lemon juice

a pinch of red chilli flakes

a pinch of Himalayan pink salt

150g mix of raw cashews and shelled pistachios

FOR THE TUNA:

2 tbsp coconut oil

1kg tuna loin, cut into 6 thick medallions

Set the oven to 220°C / 425°F /Gas Mark 7.

Combine all salsa ingredients together, season and chill in the fridge.

Blend all of the ingredients for the nut crust in a blender except the nuts themselves. Coarsely crush the nuts in a separate blender or pestle and mortar, to maintain a rough texture. Mix the nuts together with the herb paste just before applying on the tuna; this will keep the nuts as crunchy as possible. For nut allergy sufferers, just avoid the nuts and use the herb paste on its own.

Heat the coconut oil in a griddle pan on a very hot heat and sear the tuna medallions for a couple of minutes on each side.

Spread the nut crust evenly on top of each tuna steak and then place on a baking sheet and slide into the oven for about 10 minutes, less if you like a slightly raw centre.

Serve the tuna with the salsa on the side.

Salsas come in many hues, so try experimenting with different fruits and herbs. What you want is a fruity, sharp and zingy flavour which will perk up fish, chicken or roasted vegetables.

Orange chicken salad with fennel

Serves 4

2 tbsp coconut oil

4 chicken breasts, cut into bite-sized chunks

1 fennel bulb

juice of a lemon

1 red onion, finely sliced

2 cloves garlic, crushed

1cm (½") fresh ginger, grated

FOR THE DRESSING:

juice and zest of an unwaxed orange

2 tbsp coconut nectar

2 tbsp raw, unfiltered apple cider vinegar

6 tbsp cold pressed extra virgin olive oil

1 tbsp wholegrain mustard

Himalayan pink salt and pepper to taste

TO FINISH:

1 large orange, peeled and segmented

a small handful of flat leaf parsley, finely chopped

Himalayan pink salt and pepper, if needed

a small handful per person of baby leaf, lamb's lettuce, spinach, watercress etc

Heat the oil in a heavy-based frying pan on a medium heat and pan fry the chicken pieces until cooked through. Remove and reserve in a large bowl. While the chicken is cooking, thinly slice the fennel and set aside in a bowl of water laced with the lemon juice (this will stop the fennel from discolouring). Next. fry the red onion, adding the garlic and ginger after a couple of minutes. The onions should be slightly soft but still retain some bite and a good colour. Scoop the onion mixture in with the chicken and stir through the drained fennel.

Make a dressing by whisking together all the ingredients. Adjust the seasoning and add enough of the dressing to coat the chicken pieces. Serve the salad, adorned with orange and parsley, on a bed of leaves.

Pan-fried salmon with tahini sauce

Serves 4 as a main dish

———

4 salmon fillets

2 tbsp coconut oil

FOR THE TAHINI SAUCE:

2 cloves of garlic, peeled

juice of a lemon

approx 8-10 tbsp tahini paste

a pinch of Himalayan pink salt
and pepper

1 pomegranate, deseeded
(optional)

fresh chives to finish

Wash and remove any small bones from the fish and dry the fillets on some kitchen paper. Heat the coconut oil in a heavy-based pan on a high heat and sear the salmon fillets on both sides. Lower the heat, cover the pan and continue to cook, turning once, until the salmon flesh has turned pale pink all the way through (or, if you prefer, serve it slightly raw in the centre, as long as the fish is very fresh).

Meanwhile, blend all the sauce ingredients in a food processor, season and set aside.

When ready to serve, arrange the fish on a platter and spoon over the tahini sauce. Scatter with pomegranate seeds and fresh herbs and serve.

Tahini paste is really easy to make, if you feel like going the extra mile!

Approximately 200g sesame seeds
6-8 tbsp cold pressed extra virgin olive oil
Himalayan pink salt and pepper to taste

Toast the seeds in a large, heavy-based frying pan over a medium heat. Toss the seeds regularly and do not allow them to burn (this is easily done, so do not leave the pan, and stir every minute or so). Pour the toasted seeds into a food processor, along with half the olive oil, and blend until a smooth paste is formed; add more olive oil, if necessary. Season and store in an airtight container in the fridge.

Red onion, rocket & courgette quiche

Indulge

Serves 8

FOR THE PASTRY:

100g mixed nuts

150g hard, unsalted butter

100g ground almonds

100g rice flour

a little water

FOR THE FILLING:

a little coconut oil

2 red onions, thinly sliced

2 small courgettes, diced

a large handful of rocket leaves

10-12 free-range eggs

approx 120ml milk

1 tsp each of Himalayan pink salt
and pepper

Preheat the oven to 200-220°C / 400-425°F / Gas Mark 6-7.

To fit a 28cm (11") loose-based, fluted tart tin
You will need some baking paper and dry rice, lentils or baking beans.

If you have a food processor, then first blitz the nuts until finely chopped. Cut up the butter into chunks and add this, along with the almonds and rice flour, to the nuts. Continue to blend until the mixture resembles breadcrumbs, then, with the blade moving, pour in a little water until the pastry pulls together. Add more water if the pastry looks too dry or a little more rice flour if it is too moist. Chill in the fridge for an hour or so.

When needed, remove the pastry from the fridge and allow it to soften a little. Gluten-free pastries are much harder to roll, as there is no gluten to give it the elasticity it needs. You may find the pastry rolls out well, but if not - roll the whole lump into a large sausage and cut into discs approximately 3-4mm (1/4") thick. Press the pastry discs into the fluted tart tin, making sure the base and sides are well covered and there are no cracks, reserving any leftover pastry. Leave the pastry edges hanging over the edge of the tin; this will allow for shrinkage while baking. Now scrunch up a large piece of baking paper and lay it over the pastry, then pour in the rice, lentils or baking beans. Spread them out across the whole base of the tart and set the tin onto a large baking sheet. Now slide the sheet and tin into the middle of the oven and bake for at least 30 minutes or until the edges are golden brown. Remove the baking paper and its contents carefully, and, if the pastry still looks quite pale, slide it back into the oven for another 10 minutes or so. You want the pastry base to be quite brown and crisp; this will stop the bottom being soggy. Allow the case to cool and if any large cracks or splits appear, roll out little pieces of raw pastry and simply fill them in - be very gentle otherwise more cracks will appear!

Heat the coconut oil in a large frying pan on a medium heat and fry the onions gently; you want to soften them a little but not lose their colour. Remove the onions and do the same with the courgettes, then season with the salt and pepper. Beat the eggs and milk together in a large bowl and set aside. Scatter the rocket into your cooked tart case and layer over the cooked courgette. Now pour over the egg mixture carefully and lay over the red onion (adding a few slivers of raw, red onion to add colour, if you wish). Slide the whole tin onto a large baking sheet and bake in the oven for 30-40 minutes until the egg is set and the top is golden brown.

200

Roast chicken with honeyed juices

Serves 4-6

———

FOR THE MARINADE:

zest and juice of 2 unwaxed lemons

6 cloves garlic, chopped

3 tsp raw, unfiltered apple
cider vinegar

5 tbsp runny honey
or coconut nectar

2 tsp of sweet paprika

1 tsp each of cracked black pepper
and Himalayan pink salt

1-2 corn-fed chickens, cut into
large pieces

6 large sprigs of fresh thyme
(preferably lemon thyme)

Heat the oven to 190°C / 375°F / Gas Mark 5.

Mix all the marinade ingredients together and pour over the chicken pieces (a large freezer bag works well to ensure the chicken is evenly coated). Marinade in the fridge for a minimum of 2 hours; overnight is good.

When ready to cook, drain off the excess marinade and reserve. Start the chicken by setting the roasting tin over a medium heat on the hob. Add the chicken pieces, skin side down, and fry off until golden brown. Off the heat, turn the pieces over and pour on the reserved marinade. Tuck the thyme sprigs under the chicken, cover in tin foil and cook in the oven for approximately 40 minutes, or until the chicken juices run clear, not pink, when a thin skewer is inserted in the thickest part of the chicken. Pour off the pan juices and pop into a jug. Allow the meat to rest for 5 minutes then serve with the pan juices on the side.

Roast vegetable & mushroom tart

Serves 8

_____

FOR THE PASTRY:

200g almond flour

½ tsp Himalayan pink salt

½ tsp baking powder

2 spring onions, finely chopped

60g coconut oil, set hard, not liquid

a little water

FOR THE FILLING:

2 large red bell peppers

a little coconut oil

a small courgette, diced

2 small red onions, peeled and thinly sliced

100g chestnut mushrooms thinly sliced

3 bay leaves

6 sprigs of thyme, leaves picked

8 cherry tomatoes, halved

2 large free-range eggs

120ml coconut milk

1 tsp each of Himalayan pink salt and black pepper

Preheat the oven to 200-220°C / 400-425°F / Gas Mark 6-7.

To fit a 28cm (11") loose-based, fluted tart tin
You will need some baking paper and dry rice, lentils or baking beans.

Cut up the hard coconut oil into chunks. If you have a food processor, then pop all the ingredients for the pastry (except the water) in and blend until the mixture resembles breadcrumbs. Keep the blade moving and pour in a little water until the pastry pulls together. Add more water if the pastry looks too dry or a little more almond flour if it is too moist. Chill in the fridge for an hour or so.

When needed, remove the pastry from the fridge and allow it to soften a little. Gluten-free pastries are much harder to roll, as there is no gluten to give it the elasticity it needs. You may find the pastry rolls out well, but if not - roll the whole lump into a large sausage and cut into discs approximately 3-4mm (1/4") thick. Line the tart tin with a large piece of baking paper (this will stop the filling from leaking into the oven) and press the pastry discs into the fluted tart tin, making sure the base and sides are well covered and there are no cracks. Reserve any leftover pastry. Leave the pastry edges hanging over the edge of the tin; this will allow for shrinkage while baking. Now scrunch up another large piece of baking paper and lay it over the pastry, then pour in the rice, lentils or baking beans. Spread them out across the whole base of the tart and set the tin onto a large baking sheet. Now slide the sheet and tin into the middle of the oven and bake for at least 20 minutes or until the edges are golden brown. Remove the top sheet of baking paper and its contents carefully, and, if the pastry still looks quite pale, slide it back into the oven for another 10 minutes or so. You want the pastry base to be quite brown and crisp; this will stop the bottom being soggy. Allow the case to cool and if there are any large cracks or splits, roll out little pieces of raw pastry and simply fill them in - be very gentle otherwise more cracks will appear!

For the filling

Place the whole peppers in the oven for 20 minutes or so, until their surface is blackened. Pop the roasted peppers into a bowl and cover with cling film; this will make them easier to peel. Once the peppers have cooled, peel, remove any seeds and slice.

While the peppers are roasting, heat a little coconut oil in a heavy-based pan over a medium heat and sauté the courgette, onions, mushrooms, bay leaves and half the thyme until soft.

When the pastry is ready, remove the bay leaves from the vegetable mixture and scatter the vegetables over the base of the tart. Next, add the sliced roasted pepper and the cherry tomato halves (cut side up). Try to arrange everything evenly, exposing the onion, peppers and tomatoes.

Whisk the eggs and coconut milk in a small bowl, along with the salt and pepper. Carefully and slowly, pour this mix into the tart. Make sure the top layer remains exposed so you can see the vegetables. Scatter the remaining thyme on top and place in the oven. Cook for 30 minutes or until the filling sets and turns golden. Remove and allow to rest for 10 minutes before serving.

Roasted poussin with sumac & a quinoa, raisin & almond stuffing

Serves 4

———

FOR THE STUFFING:

250g uncooked quinoa

1 small onion, finely chopped

2 cloves garlic, crushed

1 tbsp ground cinnamon

a handful of raisins, soaked in hot water for 5 minutes

a handful of flaked almonds

a small handful of fresh flat leaf parsley, finely chopped

1-2 free-range eggs

1 tsp each of Himalayan pink salt and pepper

FOR THE DISH:

4 poussin (spring chicken) - these are usually very small so adapt the quantities if larger birds are used

approx 4 tbsp coconut oil

zest and juice of 2 unwaxed lemons

2cm (1") chunk of fresh ginger, grated

1 tbsp ground cinnamon

2 tbsp sumac

3 tbsp coconut nectar

1 tsp each of Himalayan pink salt and pepper

6-8 sprigs of fresh rosemary or thyme

Preheat the oven to 200°C / 400°F / Gas Mark 6.

Start by boiling the quinoa in plenty of salted water until the kernels begin to unfurl but they are not too soft. Drain and rinse in cold water, squeeze dry and stir through all the other ingredients. Season to taste and set aside.

Weigh the birds and add on approximately 150g for the stuffing. This will determine the cooking time.

Mix together the oil, lemon, ginger, spices, coconut nectar and salt and pepper to form a paste. Set up a deep roasting tin and line with the rosemary or thyme, pour in a little water and, ideally, sit a metal trivet on top to keep the chicken out of the liquid. Top the trivet with a sheet of baking paper, slightly smaller than the trivet itself; this allows the juices to flow into the pan but stops the flesh sticking to the metal bars. Rub the sumac mixture over the breast of the chicken and loosely stuff the cavity of each bird with the stuffing. Lay the birds, breast side down, on the trivet. This means that the juices from the chicken flow through and around the breast during cooking, keeping the meat moist. Roast for approximately 40 minutes per kilo. Halfway through the cooking time, turn the birds breast side up to brown. The poussin are cooked when a sharp knife inserted into the side of a bird creates a run of clear juices, not pink.

Roasted trout with chermoula

Serves 4 as a main dish

FOR THE CHERMOULA:

2 tsp each of cumin and
coriander seeds

6 cloves garlic, peeled

a large handful of fresh coriander
(use the leaves and stalks)

a large handful of flat leaf parsley

1 preserved lemon, chopped

½ red pepper, chopped

3 tsp sweet paprika

1 tsp each of Himalayan pink
salt and pepper

approx 60ml cold pressed extra
virgin olive oil

4-8 whole trout (depending on their
size), cleaned and gutted

FOR THE STUFFING:

100g raisins

2 tbsp lemon juice

4 spring onions, finely chopped

1 tsp each of Himalayan pink salt
and pepper

Preheat the oven to 180°C / 350°F / Gas Mark 4.

Chermoula is a vibrant herb and lemon marinade used often in
North African cooking, especially Tunisia, Algeria and Libya. The
flavours work well with fish and seafood but can be used to flavour
soups, roasted vegetables etc.

Start by making the Chermoula. Toast the cumin and coriander seeds
in a dry pan over a medium heat, stirring intermittently to make sure
they do not burn. Add these and all the other Chermoula ingredients to
a food processor and blend until smooth. Adjust the seasoning, scrape
into a small bowl and reserve.

Lay out each of the trout onto a large sheet of baking paper. Score
the fish gently by cutting three diagonal lines on each side.

Mix all the stuffing ingredients together and spoon into the cavity of
each fish. Sprinkle a little salt and pepper over the fish and then wrap
up tightly in the baking paper. Transfer into a large baking tray and
bake for approximately 20 minutes or until cooked through.

Serve whole or filleted with a dollop of Chermoula sauce. The fresh
herby taste complements the trout beautifully, the acidic sweetness
of the fruit and lemon a perfect foil for the delicate flavours of the fish.

"Any food that requires enhancing by the use of chemical substances should in no way be considered a food."

John H. Tobe

Salmon with roasted pepper
& nut salsa

Serves 6 as a main dish

———

3 large red bell peppers

50g nuts: hazelnuts, pistachios, pine nuts etc

3 garlic cloves, crushed

juice and zest of 1 unwaxed lemon

2 tbsp raw, unfiltered apple cider vinegar

8 tbsp of cold pressed extra virgin olive oil

8 spring onions, finely chopped

a small handful each of fresh coriander and parsley, finely chopped

a pinch of Himalayan pink salt and pepper

6 large, firm fish fillets (salmon, cod, tuna, monkfish)

2 tbsp coconut oil

Set the oven to 200°C / 400°F / Gas Mark 6.

Start by roasting the peppers in the oven until soft and blistered. Tip them into a mixing bowl and cover with cling film; this will make it easier to peel off the skin. While they are cooling, heat a dry heavy-based pan over a medium heat and slightly toast the nuts. Next, coarsely crush the nuts in a pestle and mortar or a blender. When the peppers have cooled, remove their skin and dice. Make the salsa by mixing all of the ingredients together, except the fish and coconut oil. Season and cover, then refrigerate until needed.

Heat the coconut oil in the frying pan and fry the fish fillets until golden brown on each side. Turn down the heat, cover the pan and continue to fry gently until cooked through. Serve the fish warm or cold with a dollop of the salsa on top.

Slovak salad

Serves 6 as a side dish

---

4 large potatoes, cut into large chunks

3 carrots, peeled and diced

3 free-range eggs

1 onion, finely chopped

100g fresh or frozen peas (defrosted)

1 small apple, cored and diced

6-8 radishes, sliced

2 spring onions, sliced

FOR THE MAYONNAISE:

1 tsp Dijon mustard

6 free-range egg yolks

8 tbsp cold pressed extra virgin olive oil

Himalayan pink salt and black pepper to taste

TO FINISH:

a small handful of fresh mint, chopped

Himalayan pink salt and black pepper to taste

1 tsp sweet paprika

Start by boiling the unpeeled potatoes and carrots in salted water in separate pans. The carrots only need a few minutes, depending on how small they are. Lift out the carrots with a slotted spoon and add in the eggs. Boil these until hard, about 5 minutes. Drain the eggs and allow them to cool.

For the mayonnaise
Blend all the ingredients together in a blender. Season and set aside.

Mix all the ingredients together in a large serving bowl and check the potatoes. When the potatoes are almost done (soft outside with a slightly hard core in the middle), take them out, peel and slice them and finally add them to the bowl. Stir in enough of the mayonnaise to coat all the ingredients.

Lastly, peel the hard-boiled eggs and chop and mix them into the salad. Taste, season and leave in the fridge for a couple of hours.

Before serving the salad, scatter over the mint and paprika.

To make a lighter salad, use less potato and add in some roughly chopped raw cauliflower and carrot instead.

Tamil fish fry

Serves 4

FOR THE SPICE PASTE:

10 cloves garlic, finely crushed

150g natural yoghurt

2 tbsp paprika

3 tbsp sweet corn kernels

zest and juice of an unwaxed lime

a pinch of Himalayan pink salt

¼ tsp chilli flakes

4 tbsp coconut oil

12 fillets of fresh mackerel

a small handful of fresh coriander, chopped

Mix together all of the spice paste ingredients until they form a creamy consistency.

Coat the fish in the paste and marinate for at least an hour. Heat some of the oil in the pan and fry the fish in batches for a few minutes on each side until golden brown.

Serve hot with coriander sprinkled on top.

This paste is a perfect way to add flavour and keep in moisture. Try roasting salmon fillets in a hot oven, skin side up, coated with a good layer of the yoghurt and spices.

Thai chicken satay

Makes approx 20 satay

8/10 chicken breasts, skinless and boneless

20-25 wooden skewers, soaked in cold water for, at least 30 minutes

FOR THE MARINADE:

juice of a lemon

approx 1 small handful of cashew nuts, crushed

a small handful of fresh coriander, finely chopped

2 sticks of fresh lemongrass, chopped finely and crushed

2cm (1") chunk of fresh ginger, minced

1 tsp each Himalayan pink salt and pepper

4-6 cloves garlic, crushed

2 tbsp gluten-free Tamari soy sauce

½ tsp turmeric

½ tsp ground coriander

¼ tsp cayenne pepper

120ml coconut milk

2 tbsp sugar-free fish sauce

FOR THE SATAY SAUCE:

2 tbsp sugar-free fish sauce

3 tbsp tamarind paste

5 tbsp smooth, peanut butter

1 tbsp coconut nectar

1 tsp paprika powder

½ tsp garlic powder

360ml coconut milk

60g crushed peanuts

Start by slicing the chicken breast, across the grain, into thin strips approximately 2cm (1") wide and 6cm (3") long.

Mix all the marinade ingredients together and pour over the chicken strips, making sure all the pieces are well coated. Marinade the meat in the refrigerator for at least an hour, ideally longer. When ready to cook, take out the marinated chicken and weave onto the wooden skewers, lengthwise. Grill the chicken skewers under a hot grill or onto a hot griddle pan for approximately 4 minutes on each side, or until the chicken is cooked through.

Prepare the satay sauce by pouring all of the ingredients in a saucepan. Heat the sauce over a medium heat, stirring the sauce while cooking. Turn off the heat when the sauce has thickened a little; this takes about 10 minutes. Serve the chicken satay with the sauce on the side.

Thai fragrant chicken

Indulge

Serves 4

_____

2cm (1") chunk fresh ginger

approx 8 kaffir lime leaves,
or zest of 2 unwaxed limes

1 red chilli, deseeded and
roughly chopped

3 stalks lemongrass, roughly
chopped

4 cloves garlic

a small handful of fresh coriander,
roughly chopped

3 tbsp coconut oil

2 medium onions, finely diced

1 tbsp ground coriander

½ tsp ground cardamom powder

360ml coconut milk

2 tbsp sugar-free fish sauce

8 chicken thighs, skinned and
boneless, sliced

1 large handful of coriander,
roughly chopped

6 spring onions, finely sliced

In a small hand blender, blitz the ginger, lime leaves, red chilli, lemongrass, garlic and the fresh coriander until finely minced.

Heat a heavy-based frying pan over a high heat and add the coconut oil. Turn down the heat a little and sauté the onions until lightly brown. Then add the coriander and cardamom powder and continue to fry until the onions begin to soften, about 3-5 minutes. Next, add in the blitzed ingredients and stir-fry for 2-3 minutes until they release lots of great fragrant smells! Pour in about a quarter of the coconut milk and the fish sauce and cook for a few minutes; this will stop any of the herbs and spices burning onto the pan. Continue to stir-fry the onion and spice mixture while pouring in the rest of the coconut milk bit by bit. Turn down the heat to a simmer and tip in the chicken pieces. Simmer until the chicken is cooked through, roughly 15-20 minutes.

Serve the chicken scattered with the chopped coriander and spring onions on a bed of basmati rice.

Thai seafood curry

Serves 4

FOR THE PASTE:

2 lemongrass stalks,
roughly chopped

1cm (½") chunk of fresh ginger

4 garlic cloves, peeled

4 green chillies, roughly chopped

2 kaffir lime leaves (fresh ideally but
dried is fine)

1 tsp ground coriander and cumin

zest and juice of an unwaxed lime

a large handful of fresh coriander,
stalks and leaves

1 tsp each Himalayan pink salt and
pepper

a little water if necessary

FOR THE CURRY:

100g long green beans, trimmed

approx 150g frozen peas

1 small carton coconut milk
(approx 380ml)

a little coconut oil

1 small onion, sliced

4 tsp Thai curry paste (adjust the
amount to suit your palate;
1 tsp of paste per person delivers
a medium-hot curry)

a selection of fish and seafood such
as fish fillet cut into large chunks,
and squid or prawns (approximately
150g per person)

a handful of watercress, roughly
chopped

a small handful of fresh coriander,
chopped

For the paste
Start by making the Thai curry paste; place all the ingredients in a blender
and blend until smooth. To make things easier, start with the harder, denser
ingredients such as the lemongrass and ginger, then add the rest, pouring in a
little water if everything gets a bit stuck. The paste can be kept in the fridge for
about 2 weeks, or frozen in small batches to use when needed.

For the curry
First, blanch the beans in plenty of boiling water for 2-3 minutes, lift out with
a slotted spoon and add the peas for a few minutes. Keep the beans to
one side and purée the peas and coconut milk together, in a blender, to
make a sauce. Now fry the onions and curry paste in a little coconut oil in a
heavy-based pan on a medium heat. You want to sweat off the onions and
start to release the spices in the paste, but not allow it to burn. Once the onion
is soft, add the pea and coconut sauce, the beans and the seafood. Coat
everything in the curry sauce and simmer gently until the fish is cooked,
about 5-7 minutes. Serve with plenty of watercress and coriander.

Tomato & goat's cheese toast

Serves 4

———

8 thick slices of wholemeal bread

4 tbsp coconut oil

2 cloves garlic, finely minced

170g medium soft goat's cheese, crumbled

3 plum tomatoes, sliced

1 spring onion, thinly sliced

a pinch of Himalayan pink salt and black pepper (optional)

Just a quick and easy snack and a bit more interesting than a cheese sandwich! Choose a bread you like - just make sure it's made from a good quality, high fibre, organic flour with no additives.

Set the oven 220°C / 425°F / Gas Mark 7.
Alternatively, use the grill if there is one.

Lay out the slices of bread on a baking tray lined with baking paper or tin foil. Slide the tray into the oven and bake, or grill, until golden brown. While the bread is toasting, gently melt the coconut oil and stir in the minced garlic. Remove the toast from the oven and turn over the slices of bread so the toasted side is underneath. Next, lightly brush the oil and garlic mix onto the exposed side of the bread. Add a layer of goat's cheese and top with the sliced tomatoes and spring onion. Brush any remaining oil and garlic on top of the toasties and sprinkle over a little salt and pepper. Slide the baking tray into the top of the oven and bake for 7-10 minutes, or until the cheese is melting and slightly golden.

Tomato, olive & almond tart

Serves 8

———

FOR THE PASTRY:

100g mixed nuts

150g hard, unsalted butter

125g ground almonds

100g rice flour

a little water

FOR THE SAVOURY FRANGIPANE:

150g unsalted butter,
at room temperature

2 free-range eggs, beaten

125g ground almonds

2 cloves garlic, finely chopped

a small handful of fresh basil,
finely chopped

100g ricotta cheese

2cm (1") chunk Parmesan,
finely grated

a pinch of Himalayan pink salt
and pepper

TO FINISH:

approx 6 large beef tomatoes
(or 10 smaller ones) cut into
thin slices

approx 20 pitted black olives

a pinch of Himalayan pink salt
and pepper

Preheat the oven to 200-220°C / 400-425°F / Gas Mark 6-7.

To fit a 28cm (11") loose-based, fluted tart tin.
You will need some baking paper and dry rice, lentils or baking beans.

For the pastry case
See 'Red onion, rocket & courgette quiche' page 200.

For the tart filling
While the pastry is cooling, make the frangipane. Beat the softened butter until light and fluffy. Next, whisk the egg and almonds into the butter, followed by the garlic, herbs, cheese and seasoning.

Spread the savoury frangipane onto the base of your cooked pastry and then layer round the tomatoes until the tart is full. Scatter over the olives and sprinkle with salt and pepper. Bake in the oven for about 20 minutes or so; the frangipane peeping through the tomato layer should be golden.

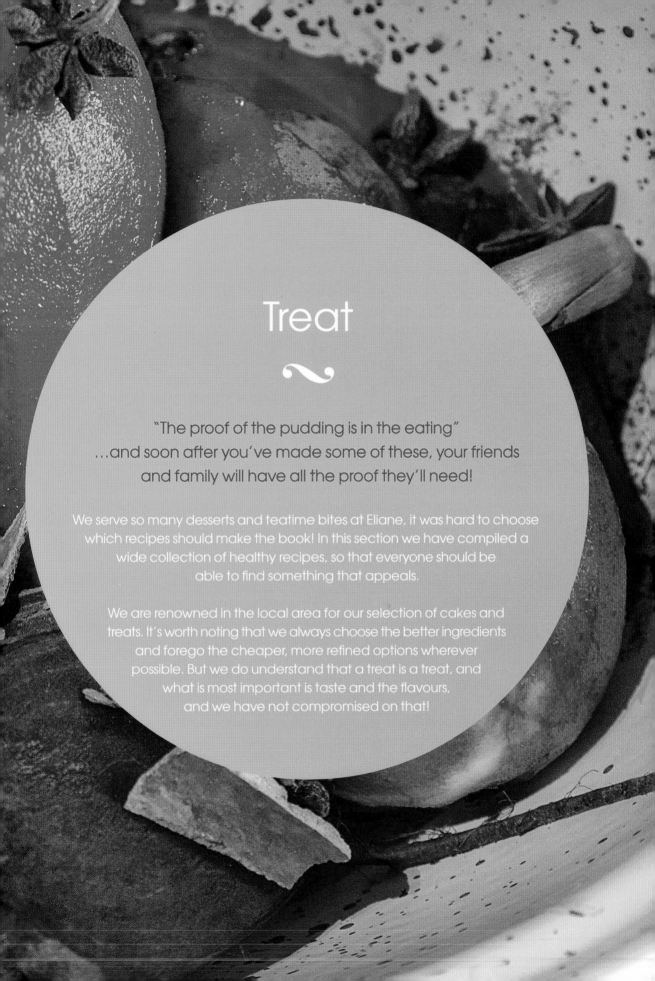

Treat

❧

"The proof of the pudding is in the eating"
…and soon after you've made some of these, your friends
and family will have all the proof they'll need!

We serve so many desserts and teatime bites at Eliane, it was hard to choose
which recipes should make the book! In this section we have compiled a
wide collection of healthy recipes, so that everyone should be
able to find something that appeals.

We are renowned in the local area for our selection of cakes and
treats. It's worth noting that we always choose the better ingredients
and forego the cheaper, more refined options wherever
possible. But we do understand that a treat is a treat, and
what is most important is taste and the flavours,
and we have not compromised on that!

Almond roulade with chocolate & raspberries

Serves 10-12

———

FOR THE ROULADE:

5-6 free-range eggs

120g coconut blossom sugar

100g ground almonds

a pinch of Himalayan pink salt

some extra coconut blossom sugar for dusting

FOR THE FILLING:

1 portion of chocolate and avocado mousse (see page 244)

approx 150g fresh raspberries

Set the oven to 180°C / 350°F / Gas Mark 4.

1 shallow baking sheet approximately 28cm by 33cm (11" by 12"), lined with non-stick paper.

For the roulade

Separate the eggs into two scrupulously clean bowls. Whisk the egg whites with an electric whisk until they form very stiff peaks. Now whisk the egg yolks with the coconut blossom sugar, in a separate bowl, until pale and fluffy. Add the salt at the end. Next, whisk the ground almonds into the egg yolks and sugar. Take a large spoonful of the egg white meringue and beat it into the egg yolk and almond mix. This will loosen the mixture to make it easier to fold into the rest of the meringue. Mix in enough egg white to achieve a spoonable consistency, around 1-2 large spoonfuls. Next, scrape in the rest of the meringue and gently fold this into the egg and almonds - a large, thin metal spoon works best. Try to incorporate the majority of the egg white, but a light marbling of the meringue and almond mix is preferable to overmixing and knocking out a lot of the air. Now gently spoon the mixture onto the baking sheet and bake for approximately 12 minutes, or until the surface is golden brown and springs back when gently pushed. Once baked, remove the roulade from the oven and set aside to cool.

Once the roulade has cooled (it does not have to be cold), take a sheet of greaseproof paper, larger than the roulade tin, and lie it flat on a kitchen surface. Dust the greaseproof paper with coconut blossom sugar. Invert the baking sheet onto the sugar-topped paper; the sugar will create a barrier to stop the roulade sticking to the new paper. Now gently peel off the baking paper. Patience is the key to stop half the roulade remaining attached to the paper! Now take another new sheet of greaseproof paper and lie it over the newly exposed roulade. Start by facing the longest side of the roulade and gently roll the roulade up between the two sheets of paper. This will stop the roulade sticking to itself and it can then be set aside until you are ready to fill it.

For the filling

Gently unroll the cooled roulade and remove the top sheet of paper. Spoon the avocado and chocolate mousse onto the roulade and spread evenly over the surface, then scatter over the raspberries. Again, facing the longest side of the roulade, gently fold the longest edge over on itself to start the wheel effect. Continue the rolling, using the last sheet of greaseproof paper to help, making sure that you do not roll the paper into the roulade! Once you reach the end, you should have a flap of paper left exposed. Make sure you have a flat platter ready and, grabbing the flaps of paper, slide the roulade onto the edge of the platter. Give the roulade one last roll to get it to the edge of the paper and slide the roulade onto the platter. Use your hands to reshape the roulade, if necessary. Dust over more sugar, if you wish, and serve.

Apple crumble with homemade granola

Pumpkin seeds are very high in magnesium, which is great for your heart. They are high in zinc, which is important for men's health and also for hair growth. Pumpkin seeds are also full of essential fatty acids which are necessary for proper respiratory function of the cells, and they also contain tryptophan - an important amino acid that promotes restful sleep.

Serves 6

FOR THE GRANOLA:

450g porridge oats
(gluten-free if possible)

120g each of flaked almonds, pumpkin seeds and sesame seeds

1 tbsp ground cinnamon

1 tsp ground ginger

100g coconut nectar

a good pinch of Himalayan pink salt

a little (3-4 tbsp) melted coconut oil

FOR THE FILLING:

4-6 large apples

a splash of raw, unfiltered apple cider vinegar

juice and zest of an unwaxed lemon

100g sultanas

1 tbsp each of cinnamon and nutmeg

1 tsp mixed spice

2 whole star anise

a little coconut nectar

50g coconut blossom sugar

Set the oven to 160°C / 325°F / Gas Mark 3.

For the granola
Start by making the granola. Mix all the ingredients together in a large bowl. Taste and adjust the sweetness if necessary. Line a large roasting tin with baking paper and spread the granola mix in a thin layer. Bake in the oven until golden but not overly brown; this should take about 40 minutes. It is helpful to turn the granola with a spatula as you bake it. This will make sure it cooks evenly and will stop it from setting into a solid lump. Remove from the oven and allow to cool, then break it up into bite-sized pieces. You can store the granola in an airtight container and use any left over from the crumble for breakfast or a quick snack.

Set the oven to 200°C / 400°F / Gas Mark 6.

For the filling
Peel and core the apples and chop into large pieces. Plunge the chunks into a large bowl of water, with the apple cider vinegar, to stop them from discolouring.

Place all the ingredients, including the peeled apples, into a large saucepan and heat gently. Cover and simmer until the apples are cooked - only add a little water if the apples begin to stick to the bottom of the pan. Check the sweetness and add a little more coconut nectar if necessary.

To make the crumble; remove the star anise, spoon the cooked apples into a baking dish and sprinkle over the granola, enough to cover the apple base. Sprinkle over the coconut blossom sugar; this is optional but does add a lovely caramelised sweetness and an extra crunch to the topping. Bake in the oven until bubbling hot and brown, about 30 minutes.

Apricot & almond tart

Serves 10-12

———

FOR THE PASTRY:

100g butter or dairy-free butter
(see page 268)

200g spelt flour (or a mixture of
ground almonds and rice flour
- 150g almonds / 50g rice flour)

a pinch of Himalayan pink salt

1 tsp xanthan gum or psyllium husk
powder (if using the almond and
rice flour mix instead of spelt flour)

a splash of cold water

FOR THE APRICOT AND ALMOND
FRANGIPANE:

5-6 ripe apricots

a drizzle of coconut nectar

100g coconut oil (soft but not liquid)
(alternatively, use 120g dairy-free
butter (see page 268)

100g coconut nectar

6-8 free-range eggs

200g ground almonds

1 x 28cm (11") loose-based, fluted tart tin
Large sheet of baking paper
Baking beans (or rice / lentils etc)

Set the oven to 180°C / 350°F / Gas Mark 4.

For the pastry
Gluten-free flour and nut mixtures are often very crumbly and do not
hold together well; it's the gluten that creates the elasticity. Xanthan
gum is a fine powder that helps to replicate the elasticity you get when
using normal flour and is worth adding when creating gluten-free pastry.

Crumb together the butter and flour (or nut and flour mix) in a food
processor. Then add the salt and Xanthan gum. Once the fat and flour
have blended to form a fine bread crumb mix, pour in a little cold
water and continue to blend until the pastry starts to pull together.
Wrap in cling film and chill for at least an hour. Pastry can be made in
advance and freezes well.

When ready to bake, remove the pastry from the fridge and allow
plenty of time for it to reach room temperature. When the pastry is soft
enough to roll out, flour your work surface and roll until approximately
2-3 mm thick, turning the pastry regularly and adding a little more flour,
if necessary. Lift the rolled pastry onto the rolling pin and fold into the
tart tin and press down onto the tin's base to remove any air bubbles,
leaving the excess pastry to hang over the edge of the tart tin (the
pastry may shrink during baking so this excess pastry will stop the tart
shell shrinking below the level of the tart tin). The gluten-free pastry may
still be hard to work with, due to its crumbly texture. Try rolling the pastry
into a long sausage and then cutting into small discs and pressing into
the tart tin, making sure there are no gaps. Wrap up any left over pastry
and reserve. Once the tin is lined with pastry and any holes are filled,
scrunch up a large sheet of baking paper and lie on top of the pastry.
pour in the baking beans or dry rice and spread out evenly. Pop the tart
into the oven for approximately 20-25 minutes, or until all the edge is
golden brown. Remove the tin and gently lift out the baking beans and
paper. Return the tin to the oven and bake for a further 10 minutes, or
until the surface of the pastry has begun to colour a little. Remove the
tin and allow it to cool.

For the apricot and almond frangipane
Start by simmering the apricots in water and coconut nectar until slightly
soft but not mushy. Once cool, slide off the skins, cut in half and remove
the stone. As the fruit is cooling, beat together the coconut oil and the
coconut nectar until completely combined and slightly fluffy. Now beat
in the eggs and ground almonds, alternating between the two.

Take the cooled pastry case and check the base for any cracks. Fill any cracks with a little of the reserved raw pastry from before. Now spoon in the frangipane mix and gently push the halved apricots into the surface. Bake for approximately 30 minutes, or until the surface is golden and springs back when gently pushed.

Serve the tart warm with cashew cream (see page 242). The tart works well with all sorts of fruit: apples, pears, blueberries etc.

For a quicker, gluten-free option, simply grease a shallow baking dish with coconut oil and bake the frangipane without a pastry shell.

Banana bread

Serves 10-12

———

450g chopped dates

4 ripe bananas, mashed

160g coconut oil

4 free-range eggs

1 tbsp nutmeg

1 tbsp cinnamon

200g ground almonds (almond flour)

100g rice flour

a pinch of Himalayan pink salt

1 tsp bicarbonate of soda

2-3 tsp baking powder

100g coconut nectar

To fit a small roasting tin, 30cm by 20cm (12" by 8") or a 24cm (9") round cake tin, lined with baking paper.

Set oven to 180°C / 350°F / Gas Mark 4.

Start by making the date purée. Cook the chopped dates by covering in water and bringing up to a simmer for approximately 10 minutes, until they start to swell and soften. Drain off and reserve the majority of the liquid (this can be used to sweeten other dishes) and purée the cooked dates until smooth.

Next, mix together all the wet ingredients and then add in the spices. Beat in the almonds, rice flour, salt, bicarbonate of soda and baking powder - if you have a food processor, do everything in this, starting with mashing the bananas then adding all the ingredients in order.

Test the cake batter for sweetness and only add extra coconut nectar, if necessary.

Spoon the mixture into your prepared tin and bake in the centre of the oven for approximately 30-40 minutes. The cake is done when the surface springs back when gently pushed or a skewer inserted into the centre of the cake comes out clean.

This banana bread is the perfect gluten-free treat. The bananas keep the texture moist and very few people in the restaurant notice that it is a 'healthy' version of this classic.

Blueberry & almond muffins

**Makes 12 small or
6-8 large muffins**

———

200g almond flour

50g rice flour

1 tsp bicarbonate of soda

1 ½ tsp baking powder

1 tsp ground nutmeg

1 free-range egg

50g coconut oil, melted

4-6 heaped tbsp Greek yoghurt,
plus a little extra if needed

80-170g coconut nectar (depending
on how sweet you want the muffins)

2 large handfuls of fresh or frozen
blueberries

Set the oven to 180°C / 350°F / Gas Mark 4.

12-hole deep muffin tin, lined with muffin cases.

In a large bowl, stir together all the dry ingredients. Beat the egg
together with the coconut oil, yoghurt and half the coconut nectar.
Pour this mixture into the almond and flour mix and tip in the blueberries.
Fold everything together but be careful not to overmix. Check for
sweetness and add a little more coconut nectar, if necessary. The
mixture should be a thick, spoonable consistency; add a little more
yoghurt if the consistency is too dry. Divide the muffin dough into the
muffin cases and bake for 20 minutes. The muffins are done when risen
and golden brown and the surface springs back when gently pushed.

For a vegan option, omit the egg and yoghurt and replace with 2-3
mashed bananas. Note that you will need far less coconut nectar due
to the natural sweetness of the banana.

Carrot cake

Serves 10-12

_____

FOR THE CAKE:

approx 4-5 carrots (200g), grated

1 ripe banana, mashed

300g coconut nectar, plus a little extra

4-5 free-range eggs

100g coconut oil, melted

2 tbsp cinnamon

1 tsp nutmeg

1 tsp mixed spice

150g raisins or sultanas

270g ground almonds (almond flour)

90g gram flour (chickpea flour) or rice flour

a pinch of Himalayan pink salt

1 tsp bicarbonate of soda

2-3 tsp baking powder

FOR THE 'CREAM CHEESE' ICING:

1 portion of soft cashew cheese (see page 242)

60g coconut oil

100g coconut nectar

zest of an unwaxed orange

To fit a small roasting tin (30cm by 20cm (12" by 8") or a 24cm (9") round cake tin, lined with baking paper.

Set oven to 180°C / 350°F / Gas Mark 4.

For the cake
Start by mixing together all the wet ingredients and then add in the spices and dried fruit. Sieve in the gram flour (occasionally this flour can clump together, so sieving is an essential step). Next, beat in the ground almonds, salt, bicarbonate of soda and baking powder. If you have a food processor I would do everything in this; starting with grating the carrots then adding all the ingredients in order.

Test the cake batter for sweetness and add extra coconut nectar only if necessary.

Spoon the mixture into your prepared tin and bake in the centre of the oven for approximately 35-45 minutes. The cake is done when the surface springs back when gently pushed or a skewer inserted into the centre of the cake comes out clean.

For the topping
Beat together all the ingredients; adjust the sweetness by adding more coconut nectar, if necessary. Pop in the fridge until needed.

When the cake is completely cool, spread over the icing and serve.

Cashew cream
& soft cashew cheese

Without overindulging on cashews, you can reap the benefits of this delicious nut. They are wonderfully versatile and are full of vitamins, minerals, essential fatty acids and amino acids. Eaten in moderation, so as not to upset an omega 3 to 6 ratio in the body, the benefits can be enjoyed in some delicious and wide-ranging dishes.

Cashew cream

500g raw cashew nuts

approx 240ml freshly squeezed apple juice, enough to cover the nuts

a little lemon juice

Soak the cashew nuts overnight in the apple juice. When ready to make the cream, drain the nuts and reserve the extra juice. Tip the cashews into a blender and add half the reserved juice. Blend until smooth, adding more juice if needed. You want the consistency of double cream. Taste and add a little lemon juice if necessary. Reserve and use instead of pouring cream; it is also great as a base for smoothies.

Soft cashew cheese

240g raw cashew nuts

approx 120ml filtered water

60g nutritional yeast*

3-4 tbsp fresh lemon juice

This is a perfect recipe for a vegan alternative to a soft cream cheese. Make a base out of crushed nuts, coconut nectar and coconut oil. Add some fresh berries and a little coconut nectar to the cashew cheese and you have a raw vegan cheesecake!

Start by soaking the cashew nuts overnight in plenty of cold water. When ready to make the cheese, drain off the cashew nuts and simply put the nuts, half the filtered water and all the other ingredients into a food processor and blend until thick and creamy. The texture should be similar to smooth hummus; if the mixture is too thick add a little more of the filtered water you have in reserve. Once blended to the correct consistency, spoon into a container and place in the fridge; the cheese will harden when chilled.

*Nutritional yeast has a strong flavour that is described as nutty, cheesy and/or creamy, which makes it popular as an ingredient in vegan recipes in place of cheese. It can also be used to flavour stocks, soups, sauces etc.

Chocolate & avocado mousse

Serves 4

————

2 large, very ripe avocados
(approx 250g)

40-50g raw cacao powder

50-60ml nut milk
(cashew, almond etc)

1 tsp pure vanilla extract

approx 80g coconut nectar, adjust
amounts to your palette

a pinch of Himalayan pink salt

Scoop out the flesh of the avocado into a blender, add all the other ingredients and blend until smooth. Check the flavour and add more coconut nectar if necessary, also add a bit more milk if the mousse is too thick. Spoon the mousse into dishes, chill and serve.

This mousse is the filling used in the almond roulade recipe in this section and also makes a great filling for a cake instead of whipped cream or butter icing. Also try playing around with other ingredients to create different flavours: bananas, date purée, mint and orange extracts etc.

————

Raw cacao has a whole string of benefits for human health. It is very high in antioxidant value. The minerals contained in cacao reduce type II diabetes, lower blood pressure and protect against osteoporosis. It is said to be an aphrodisiac and helps to combat fatigue and even fight tooth decay. Quite the array of benefits!

Chocolate beetroot cake

Serves 10-12

_____

600g cooked and puréed beetroot

500g pitted dates, roughly chopped

120g 100% cocoa powder

100ml warm, melted coconut oil

5 free-range eggs

150g ground almonds

2 tbsp baking powder

a little coconut milk (if necessary)

coconut nectar (for extra sweetness if needed)

Chocolate and beetroot are a match made in heaven. There is a natural earthy sweetness to beetroot that adds a natural sugar to the denser chocolate flavours. This cake has become one of the biggest hits in the restaurant as it is dense and rich but full of goodness - a small slice goes a long way!

1 x 24cm (9") round cake tin - lined with baking paper.

Set the oven to 170°C / 340°F / Gas Mark 4.

Start by cooking the beetroot. Puréed beetroot is a great staple to have in the fridge; great in salad dressings, to make a quick soup and obviously for baking. Cut the beets into large chunks (no need to peel) and bring to the boil in plenty of water. Simmer until very soft. Rinse in cold water - the peel should now slide off - and purée. Pop into a tub and keep in the fridge.

Next, cook off the pitted dates. Tip them into a saucepan, cover in water and bring up to a simmer for approximately 20 minutes, until they start to swell and soften. Drain off and reserve the majority of the liquid (this can be used to sweeten other dishes) and purée until smooth.

Beat together the beetroot, dates and cocoa powder. Stir in the warmed coconut oil (note that it must be warm otherwise it will solidify into small lumps on contact with any cold ingredients) followed by the eggs. Lastly, beat in the almond flour and baking powder until smooth. The mixture should be a soft, spoonable texture, so add a little coconut milk if too stiff. Taste and add coconut nectar if extra sweetness is needed. Spoon the mixture into your prepared tin and bake in the centre of the oven until a skewer inserted in the middle of the cake comes out clean (a little gooey is perfect!).

This cake is lovely served warm with a dollop of thick Greek yoghurt or cashew cream (see page 242) or cool and ice with chocolate fudge icing (see page 264).

"To know the way and not practice is to be a soup ladle in the
pot and not taste the flavour of the soup."
Jack Kornfield

Coffee & walnut cake

Serves 10-12

———

FOR THE CAKE:

300g chopped dates

200g coconut oil, soft but
not melted

approx 100g coconut nectar

4 free-range eggs

approx 150g walnuts, crushed

1 tbsp cinnamon

1 tbsp nutmeg

4 shots of espresso (or 12 tbsp very
strong coffee)

180g ground almonds (almond flour)

60g gram (chickpea) flour

½ tsp Himalayan pink salt

1 tsp bicarbonate of soda

2-3 tsp baking powder

FOR THE ICING:

120g softened coconut oil

2 shots of espresso (or 6 tbsp very
strong coffee)

approx 100g date purée, from the
batch made for the cake

coconut nectar to taste

8-12 walnut halves

This cake is another major hit in the restaurant. It is dense and moist with a perfect balance of sweetness with the bitter tones of coffee coming through well.

To fit a 24cm (9") cake tin, lined with baking paper.

Set oven to 180°C / 350°F / Gas Mark 4.

Start by cooking the chopped dates by tipping into a saucepan, covering in water and bringing up to a simmer for approximately 10 minutes, until they start to swell and soften. Drain off and reserve the majority of the liquid (this can be used to sweeten other dishes) and purée the cooked dates until smooth. Reserve about a third of the date purée for the icing and scoop the rest into a bowl. Next, add all the wet ingredients to the date purée and then add in the spices and nuts. Sieve in the gram flour (occasionally this flour can clump together so sieving is an essential step). Next, beat in the almonds, salt, bicarbonate of soda and baking powder. If you have a food processor I would do everything in this; start by blitzing the nuts then adding all the ingredients in order.

Test the cake batter for sweetness and add extra coconut nectar only if necessary.

Spoon the mixture into your prepared tin and bake in the centre of the oven for approximately 40 minutes. The cake is done when the surface springs back when gently pushed or a skewer inserted into the centre of the cake comes out clean.

To make the icing, beat all the ingredients together and adjust the sweetness. Spread all over the cooled cake and decorate with walnut halves. Note: if the icing gets too warm, the coconut oil will separate and it will curdle; just pop it in the fridge and beat again until you get the right consistency (soft and buttery). Keep your cake cool.

We've been playing around with this classic in the restaurant and have had great success using chopped chestnuts instead of walnuts. Why not give it a go?

Courgette cake

Serves 10-12

approx 4 medium courgettes, grated

300g coconut nectar, plus a little extra

4-5 free-range eggs

100g coconut oil, melted

2 tbsp nutmeg

1 tsp ground ginger

200g raisins or sultanas

270g ground almonds (almond flour)

90g gram (chickpea) flour

½ tsp Himalayan pink salt

1 tsp bicarbonate of soda

2-3 tsp baking powder

A 24cm (9") round cake tin, lined with baking paper.

Set oven to 180°C / 350°F / Gas Mark 4.

Start by mixing together the grated courgette, coconut nectar, eggs and oil. Next, add in the spices and dried fruit. Sieve in the gram flour (occasionally this flour can clump together so sieving is an essential step) and then beat in the almonds, salt, bicarbonate of soda and baking powder. If you have a food processor, I would do everything in this; starting with coarsely grating the courgettes then adding all the ingredients in order.

Test the cake batter for sweetness and add extra coconut nectar only if necessary.

Spoon the mixture into your prepared tin and bake in the centre of the oven for approximately 40 minutes. The cake is done when the surface springs back when gently pushed or a skewer inserted into the centre of the cake comes out clean.

Mango & lime sorbet

Serves 4-6

———

approx 250g of frozen
mango chunks

juice and zest of 1 unwaxed lime

a squeeze of coconut nectar

a free-range egg white (optional)

Just blitz the frozen mango in a food processor to a fine grain. Add in the juice and zest from the lime and blitz again. The liquid should help the mango to bind together to form a thick purée, but if it is still not coming together add a little more lime juice or water. Taste and add some coconut nectar, if necessary. The sorbet should be solid enough to serve straight away, but if it is too runny just pop into the freezer for 30 minutes or so. You can make a more creamy sorbet by beating in whisked egg whites. Using an electric whisk, beat the egg white until soft, fluffy and forming stiff peaks. Fold the meringue into the mango sorbet, beating in at the end, if necessary, to get it all incorporated. Place the finished gelato into a plastic tub and freeze until needed.

Most fruits work when making sorbet, but berries with fine seeds (blackberries, raspberries etc) may need to be cooked and sieved to remove them. This is a great way of making sugar-free sorbets, and the addition of the meringue creates a really creamy texture - not vegan, but definitely better for you than shop-bought ice cream!

Pineapple & coconut cake
with griddled pineapple
& lemongrass syrup

Serves 10-12

FOR THE CAKE:

300g fresh pineapple, roughly chopped

125g coconut oil, melted

100g desiccated coconut (plus extra to decorate)

180g coconut nectar

4 free-range eggs

100g ground almonds (almond flour)

50g coconut flour

½ tsp Himalayan pink salt

1 tsp bicarbonate of soda

2 tsp baking powder

A little coconut milk

FOR THE PINEAPPLE AND LEMONGRASS SYRUP:

2 stalks of lemongrass, bruised to release the flavour

100g coconut nectar

1 pineapple, peeled, cored and cut into thick batons (try to reserve as much juice as possible)

To fit a 28cm / 9" cake tin, lined with baking paper.

Set oven to 180°C / 350°F / Gas Mark 4.

Start by finely chopping the pineapple. If you have a food processor, start by blitzing the pineapple and then add all the other ingredients in the order they are listed above. This will drastically reduce the number of bowls you use! If you do not have a food processor then stir together the coconut oil and desiccated coconut in a large bowl. Beat in the eggs, along with the coconut nectar. Then stir in the almonds, coconut flour, salt, bicarbonate of soda and baking powder. Lastly, fold in the finely chopped pineapple. The mixture may be too stiff, as the coconut flour absorbs a lot more moisture than ordinary flour. If so, loosen with a little coconut milk (you should have a soft, spoonable texture). Test the cake batter for sweetness and add extra coconut nectar, if necessary.

Spoon the mixture into your prepared tin and bake in the centre of the oven for approximately 30-40 minutes. The cake is done when the surface springs back when gently pushed or a skewer inserted into the centre of the cake comes out clean.

For the syrup
Start by heating the coconut nectar, lemongrass and any reserved pineapple juice over a medium heat. Once bubbling, turn it down and continue to gently simmer to infuse the lemongrass into the syrup. Heat a ridged griddle pan on a high heat and griddle the pineapple batons until they are striped golden brown.

Serve the cake, accompanied with the pineapple and a drizzle of syrup.

This batter also works well with other fruits, especially mango. Try layering extra slices of mango into the bottom of the prepared baking tin for an exotic version of an old-fashioned upside-down cake!

Poached pears with rosemary

Pears are wonderful for improving circulation and red blood cell count. Anaemics can benefit from consuming pears regularly as they contain copper and iron in abundance. Copper improves the uptake of additional minerals into the cells. Pears can also facilitate speedier wound-healing and more efficient tissue repair because of their vitamin content and ascorbic acid, which means cuts, scrapes and injuries can be healed more quickly.

Serves 6

6 large ripe but firm pears

1 tbsp raw, unfiltered apple cider vinegar

2 beetroot bulbs

3 apples

4 sprigs of rosemary

juice and zest of an unwaxed lemon

a little coconut nectar

Start by peeling the pears and sitting them in a bowl of water, with the apple cider vinegar, to stop them from discolouring. Juice the beetroot and apples. If you do not have a juicer, use a mixture of fresh apple and cranberry juice. Pour the juice into a pan that will fit all the pears. Add the rosemary, lemon and a little coconut nectar (just sweeten the juice enough to be palatable). Sink the pears into the juice. The pears need to be completely covered, so add a little water, if necessary.

Bring the pan up to the boil then turn down the heat, cover and simmer until a knife slides into the flesh of the pear easily. The pears need to be soft but still holding their shape.

Remove the pears and wipe them clean. Serve with a little cashew cream (see page 242).

Raw chocolate cheesecake

Vanilla contains the mineral manganese among several others, so apart from vanilla being a well-loved flavour, it is also great for a healthy mood, metabolism, optimal nervous system function and assimilation of other nutrients.

Serves 10-12

FOR THE BASE:

300g raw cashew nuts

4-6 tbsp sesame seeds

50g coconut oil, melted

3-4 tbsp coconut blossom sugar (use coconut nectar as a substitute)

1 tbsp vanilla extract

FOR THE FILLING:

200g raw cashew nuts

approx 120ml apple juice

2 tbsp nut butter (cashew or almond are good (see page 264)

90g coconut oil, melted

90g coconut nectar

60g raw cacao powder

a pinch of Himalayan pink salt

Line a 20cm (8") spring form tin, lined with baking paper.

For the base
Blend in a food processor until crumbed. Press into the prepared tin and chill.

For the filling
Tip the cashew nuts for the filling into an airtight container and pour over the apple juice, making sure the nuts are covered in liquid; add a little water if needed. Cover the container and allow the nuts to soak for a minimum of 2 hours but preferably overnight. When ready to make the filling, drain off most of the liquid from the nuts and reserve. Blend the nuts into a smooth paste, adding a little of the reserved fruit juice to loosen to a very thick but spoonable consistency; think something between clotted cream and whipped cream. Once done, add the other ingredients and blend until smooth. Adjust the sweetness, if necessary, and spoon into the prepared tin. Freeze until set.

Goji berries are good for protecting the eyes from diseases like macular degeneration because of an antioxidant called zeaxanthin. The small red berry is great for detoxifying the liver and supporting the organs responsible for fertility. The Chinese traditionally believe that the nutrition afforded by the goji berry increases fertility both in men and in women.

Raw chocolate truffles

Basic truffle mix

———

FOR THE BASIC TRUFFLE MIX:

150g Medjool dates, chopped

approx 100g soft coconut oil (must
be the texture of soft butter not liquid)

70g raw cacao powder

a little coconut nectar,
approx 4 tbsp

TO COAT THE TRUFFLES:

raw cacao powder

desiccated coconut

white sesame seeds

finely chopped nuts

Raw cashew and goji berry bars

———

FOR THE BASIC TRUFFLE MIX:

300g Medjool dates, chopped

approx 200g soft coconut oil (must be
the texture of soft butter not liquid)

130g raw cacao powder

4 tbsp chia seeds

8 tbsp of unsweetened,
desiccated coconut

A little coconut nectar,
approx 4 tbsp

TO COAT THE BARS:

a small handful each of cashews and
goji berries, roughly chopped

In a food processor, purée the dates until smooth, adding a little water if needed. Next blend in all the other ingredients for the basic truffle mix until you have a butter icing consistency. The mixture needs to be firm enough to hold its shape when rolled into a ball; if it is too soft, refrigerate until it has hardened up a little.

Shake your chosen coating into a large bowl then roll the truffles into bite-sized balls and drop into the coating. Toss the truffles around the bowl until completely covered, then gently remove them and place on a lined baking tray in the fridge.

You can try adding flavours to the basic truffle mix like orange or peppermint oil and experiment with different coatings; finely chopped dried berries work as well.

Line a small roasting tin, 30cm by 20cm (12" by 8") with baking paper.

In a food processor, purée the dates until smooth, adding a little water if needed. Next, blend in all the other ingredients for the basic bar mix until you have a butter icing consistency. Taste and adjust the sweetness by adding more coconut nectar. Scoop the mixture into the prepared tin and smooth out into a uniform layer.

While the mixture is still soft, decorate with cashew nuts and goji berries. Refrigerate until set, cut into bars and serve.

Raw fudge icings

Cashew or almond butter

———

200g raw cashews or whole almonds (skin off)

a little coconut or almond milk

Blend in a food processor until smooth and buttery, adding a little coconut or almond milk to stop the mixture getting too stiff.

Butter

———

approx 200g coconut oil, this must be soft but not liquid

90g coconut blossom sugar

Beat together until smooth, taste and add more sugar, only if necessary.

Chocolate

———

230g pitted Medjool dates

100g coconut oil, this must be soft but not liquid

100g raw cacao powder

a little coconut nectar

Start by blending the dates to a smooth purée you may need to add a little water. Next add the coconut oil and blend until smooth. You want to remove any white lumps at this stage. Lastly, add the raw cacao and blend until you get a rich, chocolatey icing. The sweetness is very much down to your palate; add a little coconut nectar, if required. The aim is to reduce the amount of added sweetness over time.

Nut

———

150g soft, dried apricots

100g almond or cashew butter

50g coconut oil, this must be soft but not liquid

a little coconut nectar

Purée the apricots until smooth; you may need to add a little water. Next, add the nut butter and coconut oil and blend together. Taste and add the coconut nectar, if necessary.

———

Apricots are rich in fibre and are thus good for smooth and regular bowel function. They protect the heart from a wide variety of diseases including atherosclerosis, heart attacks and strokes. The high amount of potassium in apricots has been linked to maintaining fluid balance in the body and ensuring that energy is properly distributed to the right organs and muscles.

Raw lime cheesecake

Coconut blossom sugar is a much healthier alternative to traditional white or brown sugar. It has retained all of its properties and is actually rich in nutrients unlike the refined kinds of sugars typically used in dessert recipes.

Serves 10-12

FOR THE BASE:

300g raw cashew nuts

4-6 tbsp sesame seeds

50g coconut oil, melted

3-4 tbsp coconut blossom sugar (use coconut nectar as a substitute)

1 tbsp vanilla extract

FOR THE FILLING:

200-250g raw cashew nuts

approx 100ml apple juice

3-4 very ripe avocados, flesh only

80g coconut oil, melted

80-100g coconut nectar (depending on how sweet you want it, taste and add more if necessary)

2 unwaxed limes - zest of both and the juice from 1

a pinch of Himalayan pink salt

Line a 20cm (8") spring form tin, lined with baking paper.

For the base
Blend all the ingredients in a food processor until crumbed. Press into the prepared tin and chill.

For the filling
Tip the cashew nuts for the filling into an airtight container and pour over the apple juice, making sure the nuts are covered in liquid. Add a little water if needed. Cover the container and allow the nuts to soak for a minimum of 2 hours but preferably overnight. When ready to make the filling, drain off most of the liquid from the nuts and reserve. Blend the nuts into a smooth paste, adding a little of the reserved fruit juice to loosen to a very thick but spoonable consistency - think something between clotted cream and whipped cream. Once done, add the other ingredients and blend until smooth. Adjust the sweetness, if necessary, and spoon into the prepared tin. Freeze until set.

Sweet potato & pecan pie

Serves 10-12

FOR THE DAIRY-FREE BUTTER:

60g soya milk at room temperature

1-2 tsp coconut vinegar (less if using apple cider vinegar)

½ tsp Himalayan pink salt

130g coconut oil, melted to just above room temperature

1 tbsp cold pressed extra virgin olive oil

1 tsp liquid soy lecithin or 2 tsp soy lecithin granules

½ tsp xanthan gum or ¾ tsp psyllium husk powder

FOR THE SWEET POTATO AND PECAN TART:

approx 1kg (3-4 large) sweet potatoes, baked until soft

1 banana

170g coconut nectar

1 tsp each of ground cinnamon and nutmeg

1 tsp vanilla extract

120g ground almonds

approx 150g pecan halves

a little extra coconut nectar for glazing

Dairy-free butter

This is a versatile alternative to butter for making vegan pastry, and it is best to make this in advance of any baking you may be doing as it takes time to make.

The most important thing with any dairy-free butter is to get a smooth, buttery texture, soft but still solid enough at room temperature, not grainy and does not separate easily. There is a fat:water:milk solids ratio in butter which needs to be mimicked to create a butter-like substitute, which is approximately 78%:18%:4%. Try using different fats and milks. Soya milk works best as it curdles easily to create perfect 'milk' solids; rice milk also works but not as well. Coconut oil works well but if the taste is too 'coconuty', try using refined coconut oil (no taste). Coconut vinegar is used because it has a very mild taste but apple cider vinegar is an option - it's just more pungent. Lastly, an emulsifier/stabilizer is needed; this will mix and hold the fat and water molecules together to stop them separating - xanthan gum powder or psyllium husk powder are both good.

Start by curdling the soya milk. Mix together with the vinegar and salt and leave for approximately 10 minutes. The result should be a thick, yoghurt-like consistency.

Make sure the coconut oil is just above room temperature and beat in a food processor with the olive oil. The key to a smooth texture is to beat well and solidify the 'butter' as soon as possible, so the closer to room temperature the ingredients are the easier they will combine and the quicker they will chill. As soon as the oils are combined, add the curdled milk, soy lecithin and xanthan gum. Blend well and freeze immediately. Leave in the freezer until it resembles hard butter.

For the sweet potato and pecan tart
1 x 28cm (11") loose-based, fluted tart tin
Large sheet of baking paper
Baking beans (or rice / lentils etc)

Set the oven to 180°C / 350°F / Gas Mark 4.

For the pastry, follow exactly the same method and measurements as for the apricot and almond tart (see page 234).

For the filling

Scoop the flesh out of the baked sweet potatoes into a blender and discard the skin. Add all the other ingredients, except the pecans and extra coconut nectar, and blend until smooth.

Take the cooled pastry case and check for any cracks. Gently fill the cracks by pressing a little of your leftover pastry into them. Now spoon in the sweet potato mixture, decorate with pecans and brush over a little coconut nectar. Bake in the oven for 20-30 minutes or until a sharp knife, inserted into the filling, comes out clean.

Two little known facts about pecans are that they are rich in phytochemical substances and the mineral phosphorus. The polyphenolic antioxidant ellagic acid, vitamin E, beta-carotene, lutein and zeaxanthin are compounds that play an important role in removing toxic free radicals, thus protecting your body from diseases, cancer and infections, while the phosphorus found in pecans is vital for the growth and repair of cells and tissues as well as production of DNA.

Vegan brownies

Dates are wonderfully strengthening for bones because of their significant amounts of minerals. They improve intestinal disorders, allergies and even anaemia and are great for a quick pick-me-up snack as they're full of energy.

Serves 10-12

600g beetroot

500g pitted dates, roughly chopped

140g 100% cocoa powder

100g warm, melted coconut oil

200g ground almonds

Coconut nectar (for extra sweetness if needed)

3-4 tbsp flaked almonds

Set the oven to 170°C / 340°C / Gas Mark 3-4.

Line a small baking tin, 15cm by 30cm (6" by 12"), with baking paper

Start by cooking the beetroot. Puréed beetroot is a great staple to have in the fridge, great in salad dressings, to make a quick soup and obviously for baking. Cut the beets into large chunks (no need to peel) and bring to the boil in plenty of water. Cook until very soft. Rinse in cold water. The peel should now slide off, and purée. Pop into a tub and keep in the fridge.

While the beetroot is cooking, pop the pitted dates into a small pan, cover in water and bring up to a simmer for approximately 10 minutes, or until they start to swell and soften. Drain off and reserve the majority of the liquid (this can be used to sweeten other dishes). Purée the cooked dates until smooth.

To make the brownie, beat all the ingredients together and check the sweetness. Add some coconut nectar, if needed. Spoon the brownie mixture into the prepared tin. Scatter over some flaked almonds and bake for approximately 35 mins, or until a skewer inserted into the centre comes out clean (err on the side of gooey rather than dry). Chill (this will help the brownies keep their shape) and cut into squares.

Vegan panna cotta with passion fruit

Respiratory conditions and asthma are two areas that were studied recently in relation to passion fruit, its extracts and its peel. A mixture of bioflavonoids, which have an expectorant, sedative and soothing effect on the respiratory system, have been positively connected to a reduction in asthma attacks, wheezing and whooping cough.

Serves 4-6

5-6 tsp agar agar

500ml almond milk

40-50g coconut blossom sugar

1 vanilla pod, split in half

3 passion fruits

a little extra coconut blossom sugar

This is the perfect dessert for vegans and non-vegans alike as the use of almond milk makes very little difference to the flavour compared to a normal panna cotta.

Start by mixing the agar agar with 2-3 tablespoons of water to make a thick, smooth paste. Boil the almond milk with the sugar and vanilla for 2-3 minutes and then add the agar agar. Beat the milk with a whisk to blend in the agar agar and continue to simmer for 2-3 minutes, whisking all the time. Set aside the hot milk to infuse the flavours. Once the milk has cooled, remove the vanilla pod and pour into small glass dishes and refrigerate until set.

While the panna cottas are setting, split the passion fruits and scoop the seeds into a mixing bowl. Sweeten the seeds with a little sugar and when the panna cottas are ready to serve, drizzle some of the passion fruit on the top.

Tips: agar agar can vary, so check the manufacturer's instructions. Sometimes the agar agar can form lumps in the hot milk. Should this happen, remove the vanilla pod and pass the milk through a sieve. Tip any lumps of agar agar into a small bowl and then whisk in a little of the hot milk. Whisk until the mixture is smooth and then whisk this back into the rest of the infused milk. Leave this to cool and then pour into the serving dishes, as before.

The Eliane larder list

At the restaurant we choose to use specific ingredients,
which sets us apart from the majority of eateries in the UK.

The choices we make are based on the health benefits of each
food item we put into our dishes. We scrutinise every aspect; from where it is
sourced to how it is packaged, what happens to its molecular structure when
cooked and what healing properties it may offer. As we have chosen such
rigorous criteria for every ingredient, it has challenged our creativeness and
sent us searching for flavours that are often not found here in the UK.
Mark has been our 'go-to guy' whenever we are testing new ingredients
and is a wealth of knowledge when it comes to what nutritional choices
we can make to heal and maintain our physical health and wellbeing.

This larder list is an introduction to some of the key ingredients we use
and what the thinking is behind those choices.

ESSENTIALS:

Back to basics - Wherever possible choose organic produce and make everything yourself - no processed food! We promise you that a few tablespoons of homemade Thai curry paste will completely transform what you eat and how it tastes. The same goes for herbs grown in your own garden or whole spices ground just before you need them.

———

Chia seeds - These tiny seeds pack a huge nutritional punch. They contain a huge amino acid profile together with high levels of essential fatty acids, antioxidants, fibre, iron, calcium and potassium. They help to keep your digestive tract healthy, increase energy levels and help to rebuild muscle, which is great for exercisers. Chia seeds expand up to three times their original size when wet, so also help us to stay feeling fuller for longer.

———

Dairy-free milk - Cow's milk has long been associated with digestive problems, in part due to lactose intolerance. Increased cholesterol levels are also a symptom of dairy consumption. At the restaurant we offer dairy-free alternatives: coconut, soy, almond and rice milk. It is a question of choosing one you like, while also taking into consideration the different health benefits of each of them.

———

Go wheat-free - A wheat-free diet is becoming more well known to dramatically improve health. Even people who do not suffer from a severe intolerance to wheat notice a marked improvement to their digestion, abdominal bloating, energy levels and sleep patterns. Amongst other things, this is because modern strains of wheat are not the same as they were years ago, and many products, especially breads, have an array of artificial ingredients to prolong their shelf life. Start by choosing products made from original sources known as heritage grains, such as spelt, and make sure there are no additives or preservatives listed in the ingredients. At the restaurant we use organic bread made with a heritage grain, water, yeast and Himalayan pink salt - and that's it! We make our own gluten-free flours with a mixture of ground almonds, rice, coconut and gram (chickpea) flours.

———

Himalayan pink salt - The generic table salt we see everywhere has often been treated with chemicals, such as anti-caking agents, and has been stripped of most of the minerals that natural salt contains. Himalayan pink salt contains the full spectrum of naturally present trace elements and minerals which aid our overall health, such as: restoring correct hydration levels inside of the cells, balancing pH, helping to regulate blood pressure and blood sugar levels, and supporting respiratory health. Best of all, it tastes amazing!

———

Liquid aminos - These offer a number of the essential amino acids that we all need in our diet. Typically, all the amino acids one needs can be obtained through fruits and vegetables, as they contain them in abundance. However, liquid aminos provide an alternative way of getting these essential amino acids by way of being a wheat-free alternative to soy sauce and a useful flavour enhancer.

———

Natural sugars only - Refined sugars are perilous when dealing with health and wellbeing. We all know that sugar is not good for us; empty calories with no nutritional benefit, affects insulin production so causes diabetes and is linked to an increased risk of cancer, obesity, liver disease and now, in recent studies, has been identified as a key contributor to high cholesterol. Ideally, reduce consumption of all sugars, but, when needed, choose organic fruits as a natural sweetener: puréed dates, prunes or apricots can be used to sweeten natural yoghurt, porridge or cakes. The best alternative to processed sugar is coconut nectar (syrup) or coconut blossom sugar (granulated). Sugars derived from from the coconut tree are low on the glycemic index (GI), which means that the body absorbs them more slowly, so energy levels are more consistent and appetite is controlled. These sugars also contain vitamins and minerals which are nonexistent in processed sugar.

———

Nutritional yeast - This has a strong flavour that is described as nutty, cheesy and creamy, which makes it popular as an ingredient in vegan recipes in place of cheese. It can also be used for flavouring stocks, soups and sauces etc.

———

Organic, cold pressed extra virgin olive oil for raw dishes and salads - The health benefits of olive oil are well known, but how the olive oil is produced will directly affect these benefits. Oils not labelled 'cold pressed, organic and extra virgin' may well have used chemical extraction to create the oil. This method of extraction will render useless much of these health-giving properties (such as the essential fatty acids, phenols and antioxidants), which are necessary to aid our health. Olive oil denatures at high temperatures, which changes its biological structure. Using organic, cold pressed extra virgin olive oil sparingly in cold dishes only, will ensure the benefits of the oil get absorbed and are not harmful.

The Eliane larder list continued...

Organic, unfiltered apple cider vinegar - This has many proven and anecdotal health benefits. Many believe that it is the 'mother', and that the strands of proteins, enzymes and friendly bacteria found in this type of vinegar maximise any benefits it may bring. Many studies have shown that this vinegar, when ingested, has an effect on stabilising blood sugar levels and regulating insulin production, as well as increasing our feeling of fullness. All of these factors are very important in helping us not to overeat and in balancing our blood sugar levels. Other benefits include lowering cholesterol and blood pressure and helping to fight cancer.

Organic, virgin coconut oil only for cooking - Coconut oil has a higher 'smoking point' than regular cooking oils. This means it is perfect for cooking at higher temperatures, and that its molecular structure will not become damaged quite so easily. It is high in antioxidants which, among other things, reduce blood pressure and the risk of heart attack. Coconut oil helps to lower cholesterol, partly by increasing the body's production of bile. Increased bile production aids digestion and the removal of unwanted fats.

Psyllium husk powder - Used in gluten-free baking as you would xanthan gum, as it has similar properties as a natural thickener and emulsifier. Pysllium husk powder is also a great source of fibre. It is perfect for controlling appetite and blood sugar levels, reduces feelings of sluggishness and aids digestion. Try a teaspoon in your smoothie or porridge.

Raw cacao - Contains very high levels of antioxidants, magnesium and iron. It is also believed to be a mood enhancer, just like its not so healthy sister, cocoa (cooked cacao). The reason to go raw is that a lot of these health benefits are destroyed when heated. To make a chocolate-like alternative, just add natural sugars and coconut oil; take a look at our 'chocolate fudge' icing.

Why go nuts for nuts?! - Raw nuts (never roasted, as the heat alters their composition plus they are typically roasted in unhealthy oils) provide a huge nutritional hit: protein, fibre, unsaturated fats, vitamins and minerals. Raw nuts are associated with lower cholesterol, improved heart health, weight loss and reduced risk of cancer. They are the perfect snack, and we use a lot of nuts in our dishes - check out the raw cheesecakes; they are amazing!

Xanthan gum - Used to thicken liquids and holding together doughs for gluten-free breads and cakes. It is the gluten in flour which creates elasticity when a liquid is added. This elasticity makes for a soft, moist and pliable texture, and xanthan gum helps to mimic this.

SPICES:

We use an extensive array of herbs, spices and spice mixes in our cooking. All our spice mixes and pastes are made from scratch (the recipes for which are in this book). This helps to avoid any additives, preservatives and unhealthy oils found in pre-made products. Most of our spice library is recognisable: coriander, star anise, cumin, cinnamon, fenugreek etc. Here are a few you may not have come across:

Ajwain - A pungent seed similar to caraway seeds in appearance. Its flavour closely resembles thyme and it aids digestion.

Sumac - Is a dried red berry found predominantly in the Middle East. It has a tangy, lemony and salty flavour, often used in Mediterranean and Middle Eastern cooking. Try using it in salads instead of lemon juice or to season grilled meat and fish. It's also delicious sprinkled over hummus.

Za'atar - Is a popular spice mix used in Middle Eastern cooking. It is a mixture of toasted sesame seeds, oregano, thyme, marjoram, sumac and cumin. It adds a gentle herby and nutty flavour to dishes. Play around with the ratio of herbs and seeds to bring out different flavours.

Weights & measures conversion table

We have chosen a uniform metric system for weights and measures throughout the book but understand that a lot of people work with imperial measurements and cups. Cups are a volume method (rather than weight), to measure out ingredients. This means that there is not a universal conversion of grams to cups; it all depends on the ingredient itself. Below is a table of some the key ingredients that we use in our recipes to help with the conversion of grams to cups and ounces. We have rounded up or down to the nearest 0.5 as most scales do not accurately weigh beyond this fraction.

INGREDIENT	GRAMS	CUPS	OUNCES
Cashew nuts (whole)	140	1	5
Gram (chickpea) flour	90	1	3
Ground almonds	170	1	6
Rice flour	150	1	5.5
Spelt flour	120	1	4
Coconut oil	200	1	7
Coconut nectar	340	1	12
Coconut sugar	120	1	4
Raw cacao powder	120	1	4

Index

Heal

Maintain

Indulge

Bombay fish curry *166*

Broccoli gratin *168*

Chicken & apricot curry *170*

Chicken kofta with beetroot & yoghurt dressing *172*

Chicken meatballs with tomato & harissa *174*

Chicken with dates & olives *176*

Courgette & cheese bake *178*

Curried South Indian eggs *180*

Fish cakes with apple & mint raita *182*

Herb crusted griddled prawns *184*

Lavender & honey glazed chicken *186*

Lawar kachang *190*

Moroccan chicken salad *192*

Nut and herb crusted tuna with a peach
& red onion salsa *194*

Orange chicken salad with fennel *196*

Pan-fried salmon with green tahini sauce *198*

Red onion, rocket & courgette quiche *200*

Roast chicken with honeyed juices *202*

Roast vegetable and mushroom tart *204*

Roasted poussin with sumac & a quinoa,
raisin & almond stuffing *206*

Roasted trout with chermoula *208*

Salmon with roasted pepper & nut salsa *212*

Slovak salad *214*

Tamil fish fry *216*

Thai chicken satay *218*

Thai fragrant chicken *220*

Thai seafood curry *222*

Tomato & goat's cheese toast *224*

Tomato, olive & almond tart *226*

Treat

Almond roulade with chocolate & raspberries *230*

Apple crumble with homemade granola *232*

Apricot & almond tart *234*

Banana bread *236*

Blueberry & almond muffins *238*

Carrot cake *240*

Cashew cream & soft cashew cheese *242*

Chocolate & avocado mousse *244*

Chocolate beetroot cake *246*

Coffee & walnut cake *250*

Courgette cake *252*

Mango & lime sorbet *254*

Pineapple & coconut cake with griddled pineapple
& lemongrass syrup *256*

Poached pears with rosemary *258*

Raw chocolate cheesecake *260*

Raw chocolate truffles *262*

Raw fudge icings *264*

Raw lime cheesecake *266*

Sweet potato & pecan pie *268*

Vegan brownies *270*

Vegan panna cotta with passion fruit *272*

Introducing
Raw Respite - The Retreat

———
Mark Kimchi

Mark Kimchi opened Raw Respite - The Retreat in early 2016 - the culmination of his long-held dream to help people learn, and maintain, a programme for better eating and living practices to improve health and wellbeing.

Mark is a researcher of food science in relation to disease and is also a raw vegan chef. He consults with clients privately from his practice in Bedfordshire and regularly runs workshops, courses and corporate events teaching people how to integrate raw vegan foods into their daily intake, in order to treat the human body and accelerate healing.

In 2014, he co-founded the restaurant Eliane - in Hungerford, West Berkshire - with his close friend Rafia Willmott. Together they set about bringing healthier food options to the area, with their creativity and their passion for food as nature's true healer. With Mark's knowledge of food science coupled with Rafia's vision (and a little help from some remarkable friends), Eliane has blossomed.

Mark now oversees all the raw vegan attributes of the restaurant, where some of his juice and smoothie recipes, food creations and shelf products can be enjoyed.

Nature is the Answer launched in 2011, providing information and education through Mark's website articles alongside his private consultations with clients. Mark uses bioresonance feedback technology for analyses on health issues, and builds bespoke programmes to address his clients' needs and goals.

Courgette Pesto Spirals
- an appetiser that never fails to
please. Flavour-rich and matched
beautifully with an accompanying
raw vegan bolognese sauce.

Raw Vegan Lasagna
- a perfectly tantalising, filling and
nutritious main dish made with root
vegetables, cashew nuts, sundried
tomatoes, garlic and basil.

Chilled Butterscotch Cake
- an exquisitely mouthwatering dish
made from young coconuts, mulberries
and vanilla, drizzled with a guilt-free
raw vegan warm fudge sauce.

In today's busy world where stress and
ailments, an unhealthy diet, limited exercise,
noise, crowds and pollution are the norm,
Raw Respite - The Retreat offers a true escape where you
can relax, be pampered and learn to improve all-round health.

By concentrating on you and caring for your wellbeing with
some unique packages, you will be guided to a more vibrant
life with greater energy, creating a healthier, happier you.

The essence of the retreat is in the calming yet energetically powerful
environment - surrounded by tranquil gardens and peaceful
and friendly wildlife, resting atop unspoiled land that has not
changed in the past 500 years.

The elements of the retreat that provide stillness of mind and rest
for the body are rooted in nature and are blended with the
knowledge and teaching from its owner, Mark Kimchi
- who leads all guests through an experience
that is individual to each person.

Raw
Respite
RETREAT

The UK's most complete wellbeing offering is available at Raw Respite.
Luxury accommodation, cleanses and detoxes, deeply relaxing body treatments,
healthy raw food preparation sessions, physical activity, meditation, yoga, workshops
and private consultations - all in discussion with you.

Raw Respite's philosophy has a complete Mind-Body-Spirit approach within all its
services, including healthy eating, focused exercise, relaxation, management of stress,
learning and a respect for animal health.

A retreat stay at Raw Respite is much more than a relaxing break.
Inspired by your quest for knowledge and a desire to change, to
heal and to improve your life. Raw Respite is dedicated to guiding
you through a transformational process.

Discussing approaches that address areas of your life that you want
to change, whilst unwinding and enjoying mouthwatering food
creations throughout your stay, ensures you are primed to achieve
your goals. Delicious organic raw vegan meals and drinks are served
daily, prepared by Mark.

The retreat is energetically balanced with precious crystals and
gemstones throughout the grounds, and there is continuously flowing
water in the centre of the garden, bringing harmony to the retreat from
its centre, outwards. The soothing ambiance transfers to guests, and a
feeling of serenity and calm, makes relaxation inevitable.

Raw vegan workshops educate and prepare guests for ongoing lifestyle
changes once returning home. Classes are taught by Mark, and guests
will learn first-hand how to make and prepare raw vegan dishes that will
wow friends and family and keep absolutely everyone satisfied!

The perfect hideaway with much to share with its guests.

www.natureistheanswer.com
www.rawrespite.com